utb 3112

AF125845

Eine Arbeitsgemeinschaft der Verlage

Böhlau Verlag · Wien · Köln · Weimar
Verlag Barbara Budrich · Opladen · Toronto
facultas · Wien
Wilhelm Fink · Paderborn
Narr Francke Attempto Verlag · Tübingen
Haupt Verlag · Bern
Verlag Julius Klinkhardt · Bad Heilbrunn
Mohr Siebeck · Tübingen
Ernst Reinhardt Verlag · München
Ferdinand Schöningh · Paderborn
Eugen Ulmer Verlag · Stuttgart
UVK Verlag · München
Vandenhoeck & Ruprecht · Göttingen
Waxmann · Münster · New York
wbv Publikation · Bielefeld

Tim Skern

Writing Scientific English

A Workbook

3rd edition

facultas.wuv

Tim Skern, a native English speaker, studied biochemistry in Liverpool and London. Now working at the Max Perutz Labs, he has been teaching scientific English at the University of Vienna and the Medical University of Vienna since 1992. In 2018, he became Editor-in-Chief of Archives of Virology.
Tim Skern is the author of "Coffee House Notes on Virology" (Facultas Verlag) and "Exploring Protein Structure: Principles and Practice" (Springer).

In Memoriam Ernst Küchler, der mir
das wissenschaftliche Schreiben beibrachte:

Da hapert's! Da hat's was!

Bibliografische Information Der Deutschen Nationalbibliothek

Die Deutsche Nationalbibliothek verzeichnet diese Publikation in der Deutschen Nationalbibliografie; detaillierte bibliografische Daten sind im Internet über http://dnb.d-nb.de abrufbar.

3. Auflage 2019
© 2011 Facultas Verlags- und Buchhandels AG
facultas.wuv Universitätsverlag, Berggasse 5, A-1090 Wien

Alle Rechte, insbesondere das Recht der Vervielfältigung und der Verbreitung sowie der Übersetzung, sind vorbehalten.

Lektorat: Robert Chionis
Typografie und Satz: Michael Karner, www.typografie.co.at
Einbandgestaltung: Atelier Reichert, Stuttgart
Druck und Bindung: CPI – Ebner & Spiegel, Ulm
Printed in Germany
UTB-Band-Nr.: 3112
ISBN 978-3-8252-5066-9

In 1992, I started to teach "Writing and Speaking Scientific English" at the University of Vienna. My qualifications included English as a native tongue as well as experience of writing my own scientific manuscripts and correcting those of others. I had also given some scientific talks and listened to considerably more. That was all. I was ignorant about how to begin teaching scientific English. I had no idea about the specific problems faced by the students, whether I should take their scientific and cultural backgrounds into account or how I should go about improving their standard. Somehow, the students and I survived and profited from the first course. During that first course and later in subsequent ones, I came to recognise that the students, independent of their various scientific and cultural backgrounds, shared many common problems in writing scientific English. To address these problems, I developed a series of guidelines and exercises to turn, as rapidly as possible, the students' school English into the formal English required for scientific texts. These guidelines and exercises, modified over the years to incorporate ideas on avoiding plagiarism, form the first part of this workbook.

The second part of this book uses work from former students to illustrate how to improve the first draft of a scientific text. This skill, essential to scientific writing, is one that almost every student who has taken the course needed to reflect on and to practise. I know from my own experience how difficult it is to improve a text written in a language other than one's native tongue. I hope that the exercises will be an asset to the reader in becoming proficient in improving scientific texts in English.

I would like to take this opportunity to thank all of the students, colleagues, friends and family members without whose support both course and workbook would not have seen the light of day. A very special thank-you goes to the 21 students who responded so quickly and positively to my request to be able to use their work. Their texts add an unconventional feature to the book. Without them, this would be just another book on writing scientific English. Special mention also goes to my colleagues Rainer Prohaska, who first suggested that I teach a course on scientific English, and Hannes Klump, who suggested writing a workbook.

I would like to express my gratitude to Tanja Kostić, Brooke Morriswood and Petra Schlick whose efforts greatly enhanced the quality and scope of the book. Tanja typed in the work of the former students and was

6   instrumental in finding a way to show how the texts had been improved. She also made a significant contribution to the content and appearance of the model manuscript in chapter 4. Brooke did his best to make me kick the professorial habit of preaching and ensured that I remained steadfast in omitting needless words. Petra very carefully proofread the exercises and their improvements and put forward other numerous suggestions to strengthen the book. All three corrected innumerable errors and blunders. Those that remain are entirely my responsibility.

I also would like to specifically thank the following for their important contributions to the book: Martin Breuss, Susanne Dormayer, Maria Kalyna, Martina Kurz, Sergei Lapato, Julia Leodolter, Zdravko Lorković, Christiane Mair, Elisabeth Malle, Evelyn Missbach, Anna Mitterer, Angelika Mühlebner, David Neubauer, Sanda Pasc, Marianne Popp, Lucia T. Riedmann, Betty Skern, Marina Skern, Margarita Smidt, Lena Sokol, Jutta Steinberger, Friederike Turnowsky, Graham Warren, Philippa Warren, Junping Zhu and Melanie Zwirn.

Christian Kaier of Facultas AG efficiently shepherded the book through the production stages. Michael Karner performed wonders with the layout and remained commendably patient with my sometimes impossible requests. Robert Chionis not only carefully proofread the manuscript but also contributed to the clarity of the book and eliminated numerous Germanisms. I am grateful to all of you.

The idea for the content of the model manuscript was conceived during various visits to Cape Town. In return for this inspiration, all of my proceeds from this book will go to support Monwabisi Magoqi, a teacher on HIV and counsellor to AIDS patients in Khayelitsha near Cape Town. Supporting Monwa is a more effective way of fighting AIDS than any research I might ever do.

Tim Skern, Cape Town, August 2008

His speech is like an entangled chain; not impaired,
but completely disordered.
W. SHAKESPEARE (A Mid-Summer Night's Dream)

Amongst the feedback from the first edition were two suggestions for material for the second edition. The first was to expand on the idea that the writing of a scientific manuscript begins during the planning and execution of the experiments. The new chapter 6 grew out of this suggestion and contains more of my thoughts on this theme. The second idea was to provide support for pronouncing scientific English and giving scientific presentations in English. My hints and guidelines on these topics can be found in the DVD at the back of the book.

Alwin Köhler, Tanja Kostic, Brooke Morriswood, Ortrun Mittelsten Scheid, Ulrike Seifert and Graham Warren gave invaluable support in the development of the new chapter. I am grateful to Christian Kaier, Walter Größbauer and Josef Wagner for their professional production of the DVD, to Jennifer L. Boots for the audio file with the American pronunciation and Lucia T. Riedmann for the drawings that form the background to the credits. Very special thanks go to Martina Dötsch who was such an enthusiastic partner in the dialogue on speaking scientific English. I am grateful to the Medical University of Vienna for permission to film my lecture on "Communicating Science in English".

Tim Skern, Vienna, August 2011

The videos from the second edition are now available via the following QR code:

Lecture, Interview, Pronunciation(UK), Pronunciation(US)

In the ten years since the publication of the first edition of this book, I have substantially refined and harmonised the comments that I make when correcting the assignments of my students. The third edition takes these changes into account. Two new manuscripts in chapter 5 use these harmonised comments; the list of the comments themselves can be found in box 7.2. This edition also contains four new abstracts that illustrate specific problems that constantly recur in the students' assignments. Chapter 8 contains eight new exercises that are based on texts that I use in my class to provide practice in summary writing and data analysis. In addition, six new videos were made for this edition in order to demonstrate my approach to supporting students in giving scientific talks in English. I hope that you will find the approach useful for preparing your presentations. The first video sets the scene and introduces the speakers. Videos two to five contain three minute speeches given by former students of my courses; at the end of each speech, the student receives a brief feedback. In the sixth video, one of the students interviews me on how best to obtain a place in a laboratory for an Erasmus stay abroad. The videos can be accessed via the QR code in section 7.4.

A further change in the third edition is the absence of the two texts that were reprinted from the journal Nature. This change resulted from an enormous increase in the copyright fees that Nature now charges compared to 2011. The texts should however be available to most readers through an institutional subscription to Nature.

I thank the six students who so readily gave their permission to use their work. William Dundon and Gijs Versteeg kindly offered excerpts from the reviewers' comments on their manuscripts. Peter Wittmann and Carina Glitzner from Facultas AG provided invaluable support in the production of this new edition. Special thanks to Barbara Füzi, Ralf Jansen, Helene Mössl and Tomaž Rozmarič for their enthusiastic participation in the videos and to Walter Größbauer and Istvan Pajor for their professional expertise in producing them.

Tim Skern, Vienna, April 2019

Chapters 1 and 2 of the workbook comprise guidelines and a basic scientific lexicon that will support you in writing the English employed in scientific texts. Familiarise yourself with them and then practise their application by carrying out the exercises in chapter 3. Compare your responses to the exercises to those of former students. Look at the suggestions (sets of comments and commands with blue numbers) for improving these texts and then try to strengthen your work in the same way. At the end of the first three chapters, you should be more confident in writing formal English and able to ask critical questions about your own written work.

Taking the material from the first three chapters as its basis, chapter 4 generates a model manuscript based on imaginary experiments to illustrate how to write and strengthen a scientific manuscript. Chapter 5 proposes themes for writing your own texts and model manuscripts so that you can apply the ideas from chapter 4. Again, compare your manuscripts with those of the former students and note how they have been further modified. Correct your work in the same way. Chapter 6 offers an alternative approach to start writing your manuscripts and shows how experimentation and communication are linked.

At this point, your English should be approaching the style found in scientific texts and manuscripts and you should be gaining in confidence. It is important, however, that you continue to polish your English and that you appreciate that writing skills can always be sharpened. Chapters 7 and 8 are both designed with this goal in mind. Chapter 7 presents several suggestions how readers can continue to consolidate their scientific writing. Chapter 8 lists the pages of the book on which words marked in italics are printed. These comprise the basic scientific lexicon in chapter 1, important linking words from box 1.4 as well as a further hundred or so useful words for scientific writing. Browsing through chapter 8 and carrying out some of the exercises in this chapter should greatly increase the number of words at your disposal. There is also space at the end of chapter 8 for you to add words that you meet during your reading.

*It is well-known that, in grammatical terms, languages are more
perfect the older they are and that they always become gradually
worse, from high Sanskrit down to English jargon, this patchwork
cloak of thoughts stitched together from rags of heterogeneous
material.*

*(Bekanntlich sind die Sprachen, namentlich in grammatischer
Hinsicht, desto vollkommener, je älter sie sind, und werden
stufenweise immer schlechter – vom hohen Sanskrit an bis zum
englischen Jargon herab, diesem aus Lappen heterogener Stoffe
zusammengeflickten Gedankenkleide.)*

ARTHUR SCHOPENHAUER

The chapter begins by looking at the advantages and disadvantages
of English as the language of scientific communication, presents some
guidelines on how to write the formal English found in scientific writing
and ends by suggesting a basic vocabulary for written scientific communication.

1.1   Advantages and disadvantages of English

English has become today's language of science through historical
events, not through any inherent characteristics that make it better suited
to the task. Fortunately, English does have many positive characteristics
that make it suitable for scientific writing. However, some negative ones
also make it less than ideal. The positive characteristics include a relatively
straightforward grammar and an enormously rich vocabulary; the irregular pronunciation and the inconsistent spelling are two negative ones.

The straightforward grammar makes it relatively simple to construct
sentences. The order of words is uncomplicated and there is no need to
worry about the gender of nouns or about the appropriate ending of an adjective. Changes in the verb endings are also *limited*. Nevertheless, it is the
verbs, with their large number of tenses, that do cause the most difficulty
in applying English grammar.

English's richness of vocabulary gives writers a tremendous flexibility
in the words they can choose. Where does this wonderful richness of vo-

cabulary originate? One source lies in English's French, German and Scandinavian roots. As a consequence, English often has both a French- and a German-based word for the same thing or concept. The pairs of words "infancy" and "childhood", "judicious" and "wise", "malady" and "sickness" and "transmit" and "send" are just a few examples. A second source of variety in English is the habit of English-speaking people to absorb words from other languages. For instance, the word "robot" originates from the word in many Slav languages for work; in contrast, the words "alcohol" and "elixir" have an Arabic origin. The excellent website www.krysstal. com/borrow.html lists the hundreds of words that English has *assimilated* over the centuries. Schopenhauer was quite *correct* in describing English as a patchwork language.

In his book "Mother Tongue: The English Language", Bill Bryson states that this richness of vocabulary gives English an advantage over many other languages. He proposes that a language with a wider vocabulary has more ways to express the same thought. This may be true, but a wide vocabulary is not necessary to express one's ideas. The writer Ernest Hemingway was famous for using a limited range of words. *Nevertheless*, he was still *able* to articulate powerful emotions and describe profound thoughts.

The two negative characteristics of English mentioned above do, however, place it at a distinct disadvantage compared to other languages. The irregular and often seemingly perverse pronunciation means that even native English speakers will have no idea how to pronounce a word with which they are unfamiliar. How difficult is it then for non-native speakers to learn to pronounce English correctly? How can one explain that the important scientific words "mature" and "nature" are pronounced differently? How could a young person who had lived for a year in Hollywood as a teenager and who spoke English with an excellent American accent mispronounce the words "nitrogen" and "oxygen"? These two gases are not normally words that teenagers frequently use. Without having heard their pronunciation, it is hard to know that they rhyme with Ben and not with bean. This book is, however, only concerned with writing. A discussion on the vagaries of pronunciation can wait for another day.

Spelling is, in contrast, *essential* for accurate scientific writing. It is vital that students are *aware* of the problems. The most *frequent* ones are presented in box 1.1, with suggestions how a famous native German speaker might terminate them. Perhaps these changes will one day become reality. Until then, spelling will remain an item to be considered carefully in scientific manuscripts. One way of reducing the difficulties is to switch on a spellchecker and set it to correct when typing. Special words or abbreviations that are specific to a *particular* field can be constantly added to the main dictionary. In this way, the spellchecker can be trusted to correct spelling during typing. If it cannot correct a word, then that word will need attention. If you do not like your spellchecker to make decisions itself, turn off this option and manually check the words marked by the spellchecker. There is nothing wrong with this; you may even learn something. It is simply more time-consuming.

A spellchecker is, however, not perfect. At present, a spellchecker will fail to determine whether a word should be written in the singular or plural. Furthermore, it cannot deal with words that do exist in a language but that are used incorrectly. The thirteen sentences in box 1.2 provide twelve such words. See if you can find them. Remember to keep an eye open for such errors when you read your work.

The grammar checker of Word 2019 is also a useful tool. It *detects* repeated words, sentences that do not start with a capital letter and unnecessary spaces. Its range also extends to more complex difficulties such as highlighting incomplete sentences, marking a lack of agreement between the subject and verb (e. g. "the majority of scientists is conservative", not "the majority of scientists are conservative") and highlighting *incorrect* tense constructions.

Like spellcheckers, grammar checkers are not foolproof and are to be used with care. Nevertheless, even if they are inaccurate, you still have to work out why the grammar checker has queried your writing. Anything that makes you contemplate what you have written and consider other possibilities will positively contribute to the quality of your text.

Box 1.1 Terminating difficulties in English spelling

This text lists most of the peculiarities of English spelling and offers some humorous suggestions to eliminate them. The text circulated by email at the time of ex-Governor Schwarzenegger's inauguration and can still be found in many internet forums. I am grateful to the anonymous author. Read it out aloud to hear how it sounds!

A New Language For California

The new Californian Governor has just announced an agreement whereby English will be the official language of the state, rather than German, which was the other possibility. As part of the negotiations, the Terminator's Government conceded that English spelling had some room for improvement and has accepted a 5-year phase-in plan that would become known as "Austro-English" (or, perhaps even better, "Austrionics"). In the first year, "s" will replace the soft "c". Sertainly, this will make the sivil servants jump with joy. The hard "c" will be dropped in favour of the "k". This should klear up konfusion, and keyboards kan have one less letter. There will be growing publik enthusiasm in the sekond year when the troublesome "ph" will be replaced with the "f". This will make words like fotograf 20% shorter. In the 3rd year, publik akseptanse of the new spelling kan be expekted to reach the stage where more komplikated changes are possible. Governments will enkourage the removal of double letters which have always ben a deterent to akurate speling. Also, al wil agre that the horibl mes of the silent "e" in the languag is disgrasful and it should go away. By the 4th yer peopl wil be reseptiv to steps such as replasing "th" with "z" and "w" with "v". During ze fifz yer, ze unesesary "o" kan be dropd from vords kontaining "ou" and after ziz fifz yer, ve vil hav a reil sensibl riten styl. Zer vil be no mor trubl or difikultis and evrivun vil find it ezi tu understand ech oza. Ze drem of a united urop vil finali kum tru. If zis mad yu smil, pleas pas it on to oza pepl.

Box 1.2   Fooling a spellchecker

Word 2010's spellchecker considers the spelling of all the words below as being *correct*. Nevertheless, each sentence except one possesses a word that is spelled wrongly because it is used in an incorrect context. Find these twelve misspelled words and identify the one *correct* sentence without a spelling mistake. The solutions are given in section 1.6.1.

1. You must proof that two plus two equals four!
2. A prove that two plus two equals four is given on the first page.
3. Vaccines safe lives.
4. Spellcheckers chance the way we read our texts.
5. The theory of global warming remains to be proven.
6. Spellcheckers effect our ability to spell.
7. How do tortoises remain a life when hibernating?
8. Only a few scientists have received two Nobel Prices.
9. The affect of technology on the environment is substantial.
10. We loose the loose screw.
11. We judge how we live our lives form our own perspective.
12. The ability to write concisely and accurately is not heredity.
13. The price of the prize was a surprize.

1.1.1   British or American?

Students have many questions at the beginning of a new course. The above question concerning the English to choose for their spellchecker is the most common. A *frequent* variant, often posed by post-graduate students and post-docs, is whether American English must be used to write a manuscript that will be submitted to an American journal. The answer to both questions is that it is not important which variant of English you choose. It is far more important that your English is clear, comprehensible and concise. An editor of a journal will not reject a manuscript because the spelling, vocabulary and punctuation are from an English-speaking person situated on another continent. Setting commas in the American way or writing "sulphate" instead of "sulfate" will not affect the fate of your manuscript. Once a journal accepts a scientific manuscript for publication, the production department will use its own spellchecker and software to put the manuscript into the style of the journal.

20   If you are just beginning to write scientific manuscripts, consider using American English. Two characteristics make it easier to learn and to use. First, spelling in American English is simpler and less perverse than in British English. Second, American English is younger than British English. The grammar of American English has, as predicted by Schopenhauer, become less perfect than British English. One example of this greater simplicity is the *absence* from American English of *certain* prepositions that British English absolutely requires. Thus, the British journal "Nature" might write "On Monday, the students protested against the removal of scientific writing from their curriculum." In contrast, the American journal "Science" would structure the sentence with two fewer prepositions: "Monday, the students protested the removal of scientific writing from their curriculum." The use of prepositions in any language is usually tricky. Anything which eliminates two of them at a stroke must make a writer's life easier.

Further evidence to support the hypothesis that American English is simpler than British English comes from a comparison of the names of musical notes (box 1.3). The American system is straightforward and logical. The British system is complicated and not very informative. Three of the words say nothing about the property of the note. The word "semibreve" seems to *indicate* half of something, but it *actually* describes a full note. The word "breve", meaning two notes, did exist, but it has become obsolete. There are many other examples of illogical words in British English. Non-native speakers may even have the feeling that the team of Monty Python's Flying Circus was involved in developing British English. The habitually bizarre and unpredictable nature of British English was perhaps one of the reasons why Monty Python's Flying Circus could only have originated in Great Britain.

In summary, do not waste time thinking about your choice of English. Concentrate *instead* on the guidelines and suggestions in this and the following chapter. They are much more likely to improve the quality of your manuscript than your choice of English. Readers will remember the quality of your manuscript and its advance in knowledge. They will not remember whether your manuscript contained American or British English.

Box 1.3   Names of musical notes

Musical note	American English	British English
	full note	semibreve
	half note	minim
	quarter note	crotchet
	eighth note	quaver
	sixteenth note	semiquaver
	thirty-second note	demisemiquaver
	sixty-fourth note	hemidemisemiquaver
	hundred twenty-eighth note	semihemidemisemiquaver

1.2   Formal English, the language of science

Formal English is quite different from the English found in novels, newspapers, emails and social media accounts. In formal English, words are chosen to fit a *certain* style and are written out in full. In addition, all sentences are complete, linked together and properly punctuated. This section provides guidelines on writing this type of English.

1.2.1   Complete sentences

What is a complete sentence? A complete sentence relates a finished thought or action. An incomplete sentence leaves the reader searching for the full meaning or with the impression that something vital has been omitted. The exercises 3.6.2, 5.2.1 and 5.3.1 provide examples of incomplete or *poorly* constructed sentences for you to identify and improve.

Scientific manuscripts may, however, contain incomplete sentences as part of their title. Titles such as "Measurement of the speed of the expansion of the Universe" or "Discovery of a new gene linked to Alzheimer's disease" are quite common. *Similarly*, the titles of the figures showing the data are often incomplete sentences. There are two reasons why titles are sometimes written in this way. The first is that they sound punchier, in the same way that newspaper headlines are often not complete sentences. The second is to reduce the number of characters required. Many journals often have quite strict limitations on the number of characters in the title.

1.2.2 Punctuation marks

Punctuation marks are *essential* information signs for the reader. They include: full stops (.), commas (,), semi-colons (;), colons (:), question marks (?), exclamation marks (!), quotation marks ("") and brackets (). Full stops, signifying the end of a sentence, are relatively straightforward to use. In contrast, the other punctuation marks are often a source of uncertainty. This section contains some suggestions that should ensure that most of your punctuation marks are *correct*. Do not worry about the remainder. A journal will not return your manuscript just because some commas are in the wrong place.

1.2.2.1 The comma

Commas are perhaps the greatest source of difficulty. Life can, *however*, be simplified by the realisation that there are basically only three situations in scientific English in which commas are necessary. There is also one *situation* in which a comma is not necessary. These four situations are outlined below.

Use commas when making a list such as "u, v, x, y and z". British English does not require a comma before "and" whereas American English does. The presence or absence of a comma before the "and" will not affect the success of your manuscript. In the related list "p, q, r as well as t", neither British nor American English requires a comma before "as well".

Use commas as weaker brackets to show material that is not central to the sentence. You might want to write the following sentence.

"Our latest results, obtained using a recently developed technique, also support our overall hypothesis."

The information between the commas provides extra information which is not *essential* to understand the meaning of the sentence.

Use a comma after a linking word (that is words such as "however", "furthermore", "additionally") at the start of a sentence, or after a phrase that qualifies or introduces the main part of the sentence. This will tell the reader where to look for the main part of the sentence. For instance, look *closely* at the following sentence.

"As expected, levels of bacterial growth increased during the course of the illness."

Try reading the sentence without the comma and you will notice how the meaning changes. Here are further examples of this comma in scientific writing:

"To investigate this idea, we performed the experiment in Figure 1."

"Although these guidelines do not show every possible use of the comma, they are very useful."

"Provided that you are careful in its use, a spellchecker is a valuable tool."

Do not use a comma before "that" in a sentence such as "We showed that this hypothesis is false." Unlike some other languages, this is one situation in which a comma in English is not needed.

1.2.2.2 The semi-colon

The semi-colon should be used to divide a sentence into two halves when the second half expands upon or qualifies the first. When should you use a semi-colon and when a full-stop? A semi-colon is necessary when the two halves of the sentence are part of the same thought. If they are not, the two halves of the sentence are *bona fide* complete sentences and a full-stop is necessary. Never use more than one semi-colon per sentence.

1.2.2.3 The colon

Use the colon only in the following two circumstances. The first is to introduce a list, as the next sentence illustrates.

"We measured the following physiological parameters of competitive skiers: pulse rate, blood pressure, oxygen consumption and lactate concentration."

The second circumstance in which a colon can be used is to divide the title of a manuscript into two halves. The first half of the sentence introduces the global subject area. The second half states the part of this area under investigation. This strategy eliminates the verb and saves characters. Examples might be "Global warming: the contribution of deforestation" or "Biodiversity: the *impact* of abolishing lawn mowing". These titles are further examples of incomplete sentences that are allowed in scientific writing.

1.2.2.4 The question mark

Question marks are used frequently in scientific manuscripts because asking questions is a fundamental scientific activity. The "introduction" section to a manuscript may pose a specific question that the experiments in the results are designed to answer. The "results" section may use questions to introduce why specific avenues of investigation were taken. Posing questions in the "discussion" section is a lively way of bringing in a new interpretation or moving to a related topic.

1.2.2.5 The exclamation mark

Exclamation marks, expressing surprise or an order, are almost completely absent from scientific writing. You may need them in your emails, blogs and text messages, but you can forget about them in your thesis and your manuscripts.

1.2.2.6 Quotation marks

Quotation marks are used in scientific English to indicate that you have taken a phrase or sentence from a piece of work and have used it directly without any modification. Direct quotes from written work by another author should always contain a reference to that work. There is no law which says how many or how long direct quotes should be. If you have read some scientific manuscripts, you will have noticed that direct quotes are rare. Scientists prefer to *describe* the work of others in their own words and give a reference to the original paper. Such sentences take the form of "Smith and Jones (Smith and Jones, 20xx) reported that A is converted into B" or "Li and Yu provided evidence that X can be generated from Y (Li and Yu, 19xx)." It is a sign of scientific maturity when you can express the work of others in your own words.

Brackets are the best way of marking text that is not *essential* to understand the meaning of a sentence. Do not use a dash (–) or a hyphen (-) for this purpose. Brackets are preferable because they are directional and thus inform the reader where to look for the start and end of the inessential text.

A very useful *application* of brackets is to contain lists of examples preceded by "e. g." (exempli gratia or example given) or explanations preceded by "i. e." (id est or that is). This strategy avoids using the abbreviations as part of a sentence. Look at the following sentence.

"Anti-viral agents are available to combat several viruses e. g. HIV, influenza virus and herpes virus."

The *presence* of "e. g." as part of the sentence is considered poor style. The style can be rapidly improved by inserting the list between a pair of brackets.

"Anti-viral agents are available to combat several viruses (e. g. HIV, influenza virus and herpes virus)."

1.2.3 Write out all verb forms

There are no shortened forms of verbs (e. g. "it's", "isn't", "can't", "don't") in formal English. Remember that "it's" is short for "it is" and has nothing to do with a possessive form of "it". The following three sentences illustrate the difference.

"The powder is red. It's a red powder. Its colour is red."

If you always write out the forms of verbs, this problem will disappear.

1.2.4 Avoid starting sentences with "and", "but", "because" or "so"

Starting sentences with these words is considered to be poor style and not formal English. Words that you can use in their place are listed in box 1.4. These words are, together with the other words in this box, not just useful as sentence starters. They also serve to link sentences together and are thus a vital part of scientific writing. To support you in using these linking words, up to five illustrative examples of their use in this book

26 are marked in italics. Section 8.1 gives the pages on which these words are marked. In addition, the exercises in chapters 3 and 5 give plenty of opportunities to practise their use.

Box 1.4   Words for linking sentences in scientific writing

Do you want to add further information to that contained in the *previous* sentence? Use words such as: "in addition", "additionally", "further", "furthermore", "indeed" or "moreover". These words will enable you to avoid starting sentences with "and".

Do you want to introduce contrasting or *contradictory* information to that contained in the previous sentence? Use words such as "however", "in contrast", "instead", "nevertheless", "occasionally", "of course", "on the contrary", "conversely" or "otherwise". These words will enable you to avoid starting sentences with "but".

Do you want to start a sentence with "because"? Do not do so. *Instead*, combine this sentence with the previous one so that the word "because" leads into the second half of the sentence.

Do you want to introduce information that follows from the previous sentence? Then use words such as: "accordingly", "as a result", "consequently", "hence", "in short", "subsequently", "therefore", "thus" or "to this end". These words enable you to avoid starting sentences with "so".

Other important linking words:
Giving examples: "for example", "for instance"
Finishing up: "in summary", "in short", "in conclusion", "taken together"

1.2.5   Avoid ending sentences with "too", "also", "though" or "yet"

Using such words at the end of sentences is again considered to be poor style and not formal English.

Formal English does not contain the word "get". There are two reasons. First, "get" is considered poor style in a scientific manuscript. Second, the clarity of a sentence will always be improved by omitting "get" or by replacing it with more suitable words such as "have", "receive", "obtain", "possess" or "become". *Similarly*, phrases containing "get" can usually be replaced by a single word that more *exactly* expresses the idea. *For example*, there are several alternatives to "get rid of" (delete, eliminate, omit, remove) and to "get better" (ameliorate, improve, recover).

Here are two sentences that illustrate the problem.

"My supervisor got excited when I got some *results* using samples I got from Africa. However, she got angry when she got to know that I had got hold of them illegally."

The improved text appears much more formal when "got" is omitted (after "samples") or replaced.

"My supervisor became excited when I obtained some results using samples from Africa. However, she grew angry when she found out that I had acquired them illegally."

1.2.7 Avoid vagueness, sensationalism and exaggeration

Scientific writing should be accurate, appropriate and measured. To achieve greater accuracy, eliminate words such as "a lot", "a bit" and "a little" in scientific writing. They have no value. Alternatives for "a lot" include: "several", "many", "certain", "numerous", "considerable", "a plethora", "a panoply". Find your own alternatives for "a bit" and "a little" using the resources given in section 7.1.

Make your scientific writing appropriate by avoiding adjectives such as "amazing", "incredible", "unbelievable", "stunning" or "spectacular". *In addition*, do not end sentences with exclamation marks.

Absolute statements (e.g. "This hypothesis will never be falsified.") and exaggerated accuracy (e.g. "Our results provide 100% proof of our theory.") have no place in measured scientific writing.

Emails and text messages are slowly leading the way to the elimination of "a" and "the" from the English language. Until they disappear completely, it is important to use them correctly in scientific English. *In addition*, their use often presents a special problem for those whose first language lacks such words. This includes speakers of Chinese, Japanese, the Slav languages and most African languages.

Box 1.5 presents some guidelines for their use. The three sentences below illustrate the use of the guidelines.

"During his voyages, Darwin noticed *variation* in animals. He became interested in a variation in the beaks of finches. Only a scientist with Darwin's background could have noticed the variation in these birds."

The word "variation" appears once in each sentence. In its first *appearance*, it is not preceded by "a" or "the" because it is a universal concept (guideline 3). In the second sentence, "variation" is preceded by "a" because the variation in the beaks is just one of many that Darwin observed (guideline 1). In the third sentence, "variation" is preceded by "the" because the variation is the specific one referred to in the second sentence (guideline 2).

Box 1.6 provides a further opportunity to practise using the guidelines for "the" and "a".

Box 1.5   Guidelines for using "the" and "a"

1. If you use a word to refer to something that is common (to be strictly accurate, something that occurs more than once in the universe), you will need to put "a" in front of that word. If the word begins with a vowel, you will need "an". "A" and "an" are never used before words in the plural. Examine the use of "a" and "an" in the sentences below.

"There is a big mess on my desk."

"We did an experiment to verify this."

There are many messes on many desks in the universe. Many experiments are done every day.

2. You always need "the" if the thing you are referring to is specific, even though there are many of them. The following sentences follow on from those above.

"The big mess on my desk is growing."

"The experiment verified our hypothesis."

The mess and the experiment were specified in the sentences above. This excludes all other messes and experiments, wherever they are and whenever they occurred.

3. You do not need "a" or "the" at all if the word you are using covers a universal concept or has a general meaning.

"Messes are often interesting."

"Experiments form the basis of science."

4. Some words that are universal concepts can also be used specifically and therefore require "the". The word "hygiene" is a good example.

"Hygiene is important in hospitals."

"The hygiene in the old hospital is poor."

5. You do not need "a" or "the" if a word indicating possession (e. g. "my, its, their") precedes the thing you are describing.

Box 1.6   Practising the use of the articles "the" and "a" in English

The text below is based on an abstract written by a student whose first language does not use this type of article. The original has been modified to make it more accessible, whilst keeping the errors in the use of "the" and "a". The *idea* of "patient-specific design of medicines" is fictitious but it fits well with the original text. Read the text, concentrating on the position and presence or *absence* of the articles "the" and "a". Some are used correctly, some used incorrectly. *Occasionally*, an article is missing completely. Each sentence needs at least one correction. Use the guidelines to decide how to improve the text. My suggestions are to be found in section 1.6.2.

Patient-specific design of medicines (PSDM) is novel method which was first described by Smith and Jones. PSDM method is based on the conventional designs modified by using alternative gene-based protocol. Main feature of the PSDM approach is its high specificity of treatment. The principle of the PSDM approach is depicted in the Figure 1.

Using PSDM method, we observe the shift in the specificity of the treatment. During the normal design of medicines, specificity is obtained from experience of the scientists. In the PSDM method, the specificity is obtained from the genes of the patient. Specificity of the PSDM method can be *augmented* by adding information from the family members. The PSDM method is *estimated* to increase specificity by factor of five.

Words don't come easy.
F. R. DAVID

The English language has, as mentioned in section 1.1, a rich vocabulary. Nevertheless, box 1.7 presents a suggestion for a basic scientific lexicon that contains only about 200 of the thousands of words available. Learn the meaning of these words and use them actively in your writing. If you can exploit the words from this lexicon, your scientific writing will rapidly become stronger and more mature.

The majority of the words from the basic scientific lexicon were used in writing this book. Up to five illustrative examples of their use in this book are marked in italics. Section 8.2 provides the pages on which the marked words can be found. If the use of a word in this book does not make its meaning clear, refer to a dictionary or a thesaurus.

An alternative approach to finding the meaning of a word from box 1.7 is to look for words in scientific databases. Examples of these databases include PubMed (www.pubmed.gov) or Google Scholar (scholar.google. com); others are listed in section 7.1. Searching these databases for an unknown word will provide you with many articles that have your word of interest in the title or in the abstract. From these, you should be *able* to obtain *hints* on the meaning of the word and see how it is used in scientific writing. As an exercise, try to determine the meaning of the important scientific words "purport", "pinpoint", "feasible", "plausible" and "flaw" by typing them into PubMed. Actively investigating the meaning of words in this way will help you to use them more regularly in your own writing.

Box 1.7   A basic lexicon for scientific writing

Verbs		**Nouns**
accumulate	interest	absence
adapt	invent	activation
affect	investigate	analysis
ask	judge	answer
assay	maintain	appearance
attempt	observe	application
cause	oppose	attempt
cite	pinpoint	background
compare	point to	blank
conclude	propose	cause
confirm	prove	chance
confuse	purport	change
consider	quantify	citation
correlate	quote	clue
decline	record	component
decrease	remain	condition
deduce	repeat	conflict
demonstrate	reproduce	consequence
describe	require	constant
destroy	screen	control
detect	search	curve
deteriorate	shed light on	data
disprove	show	decrease
disturb	solve	difference
document	strengthen	discovery
evidence	suggest	discrepancy
explain	support	distribution
falsify	survive	dose-response
find	test	effect
follow	treat	enigma
illustrate	try	equilibrium
increase	underline	event
indicate	vary	evidence
induce	verify	exclusion
infer	work	experiment

figure
flaw
function
graph
hint
hypothesis
idea
illustration
image
inclusion
increase
incubation
ingredient
input
interaction
level
mechanism
mock
model
mystery
observation
panel
paradox
parameter
participant
pathway
performance
period
possibility
prerequisite
presence
process
product
question
ratio
reason
relevance
report

research
result
role
signal
situation
solution
specificity
structure
synthesis
table
target
theory
variable
variation
variety
version
volunteer
work

Adjectives and adverbs
able
active
actually
affected
artificial
associated
aware
capable
certain
closely
consistent
contradictory
correct
dependent
detrimental
essential
exactly
exclusively

external
feasible
frequent
incorrect
internal
inversely
likely
limited
linear
multiple
necessary
noteworthy
particular
pertinent
plausible
poorly
previous
prior
proportional
putative
random
relevant
resistant
robust
severe
significant
similarly
simultaneous
unable
variable

▮ Use a spellchecker
▮ Use formal English
▮ Use linking words
▮ Use words from a basic scientific lexicon

1.5   References

Books
Bryson, B. (1990) Mother Tongue: The English Language.

Websites
http://scholar.google.com
www.krysstal.com/borrow.html
www.pubmed.gov

1.6   Improvements to exercices

1.6.1   Solutions to box 1.2 "Fooling a spellchecker"

1. You must prove that two plus two equals four!
2. A proof that two plus two equals four is given on the first page.
3. Vaccines save lives.
4. Spellcheckers change the way we read our texts.
5. The theory of global warming remains to be proven.
6. Spellcheckers affect our ability to spell.
7. How do tortoises remain alive when hibernating?
8. Only a few scientists have received two Nobel Prizes.
9. The effect of technology on the environment is substantial.
10. We lose the loose screw.
11. We judge how we live our lives from our own perspective.
12. The ability to write concisely and accurately is not hereditary.
13. The price of the prize was a surprise.

The patient-specific design of medicines (PSDM) is a novel method which was first described by Smith and Jones. The PSDM method is based on conventional designs modified by using an alternative gene-based protocol. The main feature of the PSDM approach is its high specificity of treatment. The principle of the PSDM approach is depicted in Figure 1.

Using the PSDM method, we *observe* a shift in the specificity of the treatment. During the normal design of medicines, specificity is obtained from the experience of the scientists. In the PSDM method, specificity is obtained from the genes of the patient. The specificity of the PSDM method can be augmented by adding information from family members. The PSDM method is estimated to increase *specificity* by a factor of five.

Put it before them briefly so that they will read it.
Clearly so they will appreciate it.
Picturesquely so they will remember it.
And, above all, accurately so they will be guided by its light.
JOSEPH PULITZER

This chapter contains eight guidelines specifically designed to transform school or college English into scientific English. Although the guidelines were selected with non-native speakers in mind, they are also helpful to native speakers. Remember that English as a first language is not a passport to writing clear scientific English. *Indeed*, non-native speakers who master this chapter may be on the way to writing better scientific English than native speakers.

Any book on how to write good English is *certain* to contain seven of the guidelines. The one exception, the guideline "Omit needless words!", is unique to the book "The Elements of Style" by W. Strunk, Jr. and E. B. White. This book, first published in 1918 and still in print, remains the best book available on writing good English. Its 105 pages can now be accessed for free at www.bartleby.com/141.

2.1   Eight guidelines for improving your writing technique

The eight guidelines are discussed in detail in the sections 2.1.1 to 2.1.8. The accompanying exercises as well as those in chapter 3 are designed to help you gain experience in applying the guidelines. Chapter 5 provides further opportunities for practice.

2.1.1   Make a plan

A plan is *essential* for any piece of writing. Before writing, divide the work into sections. For each section, make a list of the *relevant* points to be included and order them according to themes. Each of these themes can then be developed later into a paragraph. *For instance*, in the introduction to a scientific manuscript, the relevant points might be the overall field in which your interest lies, the specific area that you are working on and the question that you addressed. Each of these points would form the basis of one or more paragraphs in the introduction.

The plan should give an initial overview of how the work will look after writing. Naturally, the plan cannot account for all contingencies and may have to be modified to accommodate insertions and deletions as well as extensive rearrangement of the text.

2.1.2 Use a clean and legible layout

A clean and legible layout is vital to the success of written work. A *poorly* laid out piece of work may discourage the reader and prevent him or her from discovering its contents. The following five simple suggestions for a clean and legible layout of an A4 page are based on the requirements of the majority of scientific journals for the preparation of manuscripts.

▌ Use double-spaced text
This stops the text from appearing crowded and allows the reader to write comments and corrections between the lines.

▌ Use justified format
This makes the text fit to the page margins. *Consequently*, the reader's eye does not have to permanently adjust to a different line length.

▌ Use 12 point text with Arial or Helvetica as your standard font
In my opinion, Arial and Helvetica are fonts that are easy to read and are available on almost every computer. *In contrast*, Times Roman is much more tiring to read because the letters have different widths and thicknesses. Calibri, the default font of Word 2010, is also acceptable.

▌ Indent your paragraphs
To indent means to move the first line of a paragraph inwards.

▌ Use sub-headings
Using sub-headings in a long block of text informs the reader that the author is introducing a new topic.

A paragraph is a collection of sentences on the same theme or topic. A paragraph can consist of just a single sentence, although this is unusual. Using paragraphs to collect ideas is the foundation of all writing. If you cannot use them, your thoughts will be incoherent and you will be *unable* to communicate them to other scientists.

The *previous* section recommended marking the start of a paragraph by indenting the first line. In your A4 manuscript, the indent should be at least one centimetre; *otherwise*, the start of the paragraph may not stand out clearly. An alternative option is to leave a blank line between para-graphs. *However*, be *aware* that if a blank line falls between two pages, the start of the paragraph may easily be overlooked.

A curious problem with paragraph *structure* has arisen with the wide-spread use of word-processing software. The problem stems from the sym-bol for a paragraph (¶), introduced with the "enter" or "return" key. This symbol should only be used at the end of a paragraph. A *significant* minor-ity of students erroneously use this symbol at the end of each sentence.

If you are unsure about constructing paragraphs, the exercises in chap-ters 3 and 5 are designed to help you use them. Learn to recognise para-graphs by examining their structure in newspapers or journals. In your own writing, you should always ask yourself whether the paragraphs are correctly assembled and clearly mark all paragraphs requiring improve-ment.

2.1.4   Write simple sentences

> *Sometimes one has difficult things to say,*
> *but one ought to say them as simply as one knows how.*
> G. H. HARDY

Simple sentences are the best way to express complex thoughts. If you are just starting out and English is not your first language, you may find it difficult to control the length of your sentences. If your first language is German, you may have a natural tendency to write sentences of obscene length. It is important that you put this tendency away when you write in English.

I offer two pieces of advice to students who have problems constructing simple sentences. First, use only one idea per sentence. Second, write your sentences as direct or straightforward statements. Such sentences (like this one) have the subject at the start. The verb and the object follow straight away. There is no long, explanatory phrase at the beginning of a direct sentence. There is no marginal information somewhere in the middle.

Another way to find out about direct sentences is to listen to how people talk to each other. People talk in short sentences, even in German. One of the secrets of the most *able* science writers is that they write as if they were speaking to the reader. This automatically leads them to use simple, straightforward sentences. Jacob Bronowski's wonderful book "The Ascent of Man" is a fine example. In the videos that accompany this book, two of the students very effectively empahsise this point by speaking in short, clear sentences (see section 7.4).

Box 2.1 provides you with four sentences that are too long. Can you split them into two? Section 2.5.1 has some suggestions.

Writing short, straightforward sentences is a starting point. *Of course,* it is *necessary* to add minor points or to qualify the content of a sentence in scientific writing. *For instance,* a common construction to qualify the content in scientific writing is the escape route or disclaimer. In this construction, a scientist first makes a clear statement. A second part then follows, indicating that the statement is probably not true for every *situation. For example, consider* the following two sentences which a virologist might hopefully write one day.

"We have developed a vaccine against HIV. However, we have not yet tested it against all known strains of HIV."

The second sentence qualifies the direct statement in the first. This allows the scientist to escape in case the vaccine is not universally applicable. The meaning is clearly expressed by the two sentences. However, combining the sentences connects the qualification or escape route more *closely* with the first sentence.

"We have developed a vaccine against HIV, although we have not yet tested it against all known strains of HIV."

With more practice and experience, you can begin to construct sentences with more than one idea and qualify statements with one sentence as above. Always keep in mind, though, that simpler sentences are generally more manageable.

Box 2.1   Shortening sentences by splitting them into two

These four sentences are too long and should be split into shorter ones. What would you suggest? Compare your ideas with mine in section 2.5.1.

1. To be a good scientist, you have to be tolerant and patient when experiments or interpretations do not turn out as you had predicted, you must be able to stand high levels of frustration.
2. 62% of certified drug addicts believe that cannabis has effects on the behaviour of car drivers and machine operators which lengthen their reaction time, 45% of students shared this opinion and only 38% of customers interviewed at discotheques were *aware* of this negative effect of cannabis.
3. Finally, the correlation has been clearly shown, even though not all parameters have as yet been investigated and further investigations have to be done.
4. This results in texts which are extremely difficult to read as well as revealing to the world that their authors are clueless about paragraph structure.

2.1.5   Write positive sentences

What is the difference between positive and negative sentences? Negative sentences contain words such as "no", "not", "none", "nor", "nothing" and "never". Positive sentences lack these words. Generally, positive sentences are easier to understand and more simple to construct than negative ones. Compare the following two *versions* of the same thought.

"Scientists for whom English is not their first language should not be at a disadvantage."

"Scientists for whom English is a second language should have the same status as native speakers."

Which was simpler to construct? Which do you think is more comprehensible? Box 2.2 gives you ten further examples to practise turning negative sentences into positive ones.

Here is another example with two negatives taken from the preface (p. xvi) to Fintan O'Toole's excellent treatise "Heroic Failure" on how Brexit came about.

"Nor does this purport to be a profound analysis of the economic dislocations and insecurities without which English unhappiness could not have had such a dramatic result."

Even the lady at the publisher who gave me permission to use the sentence agreed that this is quite a sentence. Here is a clearer version without any negatives.

"This (book) also avoids an analysis of the economic dislocations and insecurities that allowed English unhappiness to have such a dramatic result".

Which version do you think is clearer? I also selected this sentence because it introduces you to the word "purport", often used in science instead of pretend. "Purport" is often found in the introduction to an unfavourable review of a manuscript as in the following imaginary example.

"This manuscript purports to show a relationship between A and B. However, the manuscript fails to achieve this goal for the following reasons."

If you are still unsure about the meaning of this word, you can find examples of its use by searching PubMed for abstracts that contain it.

I have tried to write positive sentences in this book. Clearly, it is impossible to permanently avoid negative words, so that there are quite a few negative sentences. It is just something to keep in mind. Check your work for complex negative sentences and try to keep them to a minimum.

Box 2.2 Positive and negative sentences

Turn the following negative sentences into positive ones. They contain most of the standard negative constructions used in English. You may find some of the following words useful: absent, avoid, constant, contain, fail, ignore, lack, overlook, questionable, resistant. My suggestions can be found in section 2.5.2.

1. The experiment did not work.
2. No changes were observed in any of the variables tested.
3. There is not a piece of evidence supporting this hypothesis.
4. The variation was never more than 1%.
5. None of the alternative explanations seemed *likely*.
6. Neither the fear of global warming nor the number of fatal accidents influence car drivers.
7. Nothing is dangerous about this method.
8. No-one noticed the discrepancy between the two sets of data.
9. In none of the samples could the desired compound be found.
10. No less than eleven substances were present in the mixture.

2.1.6 Write active sentences

What is the difference between *active* and passive sentences? "We mixed A and B" is an active sentence. "A and B were mixed together" is the passive version. Active sentences are more direct, shorter and clearer. Compare the following two versions of the same thought.

"The ability of the antibiotics to inhibit bacterial growth was examined by using standard *techniques*." (15 words)

"We used standard techniques to examine the ability of antibiotics to inhibit bacterial growth." (14 words)

The active sentence is much clearer. Here is another example, based on a sentence frequently found in scientific writing. Once again, the active version is preferable.

"The improved versions are presented in section x." (8 words)

"Section x presents the improved versions." (6 words)

Another motive for writing active sentences is that they are more natural. We do not speak in the passive. If you do not believe me, try explaining what you did today in the passive. "Coffee was drunk at breakfast. Afterwards, teeth were brushed." Relating daily experiences in this way is not natural. Why then should we use the passive for scientific writing?

It is your decision whether you use more active sentences than passive ones. If you think you can transmit your thoughts better using passive sentences, then go ahead. Just remember though that good writing should sound as if you are speaking to someone.

2.1.7 Omit needless words

As mentioned at the beginning of this chapter, the command "Omit needless words!" originates from the book "The Elements of Style". This concept of removing superfluous words often comes as a surprise to some students. Many share the conviction that high-class scientific writing requires numerous complicated words. The most productive step for such students on the path to writing more concisely is to abandon this belief.

Recognising and removing unnecessary words is, like many skills in writing, a question of practice. Several exercises in this book provide that practice and enable you to build up the experience to *judge* whether a word, a phrase, a sentence or a paragraph may be *superfluous*. As an example, examine the following two sentences.

"The fact that many young scientists need a *significant* amount of practice to improve their written communication skills is a case in point. It can be seen from the diagram in Figure 1 that those students who regularly handed in written work performed at a higher level than those who did not."

The words at the beginning of the two sentences are typical phrases which turn up in scientific writing but which do not add to the meaning. The shortened versions are much more effective.

"Many young scientists need practice to improve their writing. Figure 1 shows that students who wrote regularly performed better."

Discussion in class with my students on writing active or passive sentences invariably leads to the question whether it is acceptable to use "I" or "We" in scientific writing. Clearly, if I encourage the use of the active voice, I must also accept the use of first person pronouns. What about the scientific community as a whole? Ken Hyland and Kevin Jiang (2017) have provided data to answer this question. The authors noted an increase in the use of "I" and "We" in recent years in the natural sciences but less so in the social sciences. Thus, such sentences at least in the natural sciences are becoming more commonplace. My advice to my students at the end of the class discussions is pragmatic. If the writer feels that the clarity of the sentence benefits from "I" or "we", then their use is justified.

Box 2.3 has a further six sentences with many needless words. Section 2.5.3 presents the improved versions.

Box 2.3   Omit needless words!

Rewrite the sentences to make them simpler. See how many words you can remove. My suggestions can be found in section 2.5.3.

1. It can be seen from Figure 1 that there is a significant correlation between the rate of growth of the incidence of cardiac-related disease and illness and the increasing frequency of the possession and use of a television.
2. It is a fact that 20% of the world's population has no clean water or enough to eat.
3. The effect of compound X on blood pressure has not yet been investigated in any detail.

4. Another important reason for this optimisation is the fact that we should try to get rid of pollution.
5. Synergy will lead to a *significant* reduction in the amount of funding required.
6. There is a considerable, if not extensive, body of literature dedicated to demonstrating that the Earth can be considered as a spherical body traversing a circular path around a similarly shaped, although significantly larger and completely different in nature, body which is in common parlance termed the Sun.

2.1.8 Read and think about your work

If you have not read your *work*, why should anyone else? Do this on a printout as errors, inconsistencies and discrepancies are often very difficult to *detect* on the computer screen. *In addition*, the printout lets you compare different pages. This is very time-consuming on the monitor. *For instance*, if there are two abbreviations for the same chemical in various parts of the manuscript, it will be very difficult to *find* this *inconsistency* on the monitor.

Reading your work is only the first step toward improving it. You must also start to think critically about it. Put your writing into question. Does the text fit together? Read it out aloud to find out. Are the sentences too complex? Read them aloud to find out. Is the text written in formal English? Look at chapter 1 to check. Did you keep the guidelines from chapter 2 in mind whilst writing? Search again for complicated sentences and needless words. Simplify the sentences and omit the needless words. Did you think about the reader whilst writing? Do all the sentences express your thoughts so that the reader will understand them? These questions are the first steps on the way to writing a coherent text in scientific English. Box 3.2 has further suggestions to help you identify problems in written work.

2.2 Just to make you feel better

> *Do as I say, not as I do!*
> CHILD-REARERS' ADAGE

The first two chapters contained a plethora of guidelines and suggestions for scientific English. You are perhaps wondering how long it will take to grasp their use and whether you will be *able* to apply them to every text you write. My advice is not to worry for now. Just try as much as you

46 can to use them in your writing. The more you practise, the more they will come automatically.

should be revised by a native speaker. Presumably, the reviewers did not expect well-written English manuscripts from Viennese scientists. These native English speakers included a fellow of the Royal Society, a former chair of the EMBO Science & Society Committee and me. Thus, if a reviewer suggests English revision you are in good company! In each of the three cases above, we all simply wrote back that the English had been checked by a native speaker (which was true) without making any language changes. This course of action has also been recommended by Janet Carter-Sigglow (1997), working in the translation centre of a research institution in Germany.

In short, if you receive unpleasant remarks about your level of English, do not despair. Read through your text again and see whether the reviewer is correct. Obtain the opinion of an English native-speaker and accept their comments. If they agree with the reviewer, then your manuscript will have been improved; if not, then you can write back in the way that I mentioned in the last paragraph.

Finally, reviewers themselves are also human. Here are two reviewers' comments on the standard of English in two manuscripts written and/or read by English native speakers.

"Finally if authors should improve their English lnguage that will be helpful."

(The misspelling of the word "language" was in the original comment)

"This study is better to understand the concepts of how they determine protein degradation in some proteins. The data are interesting, however it is not suitable for publication unless language extensively was edited."

Both manuscripts were not surprisingly returned to the journals concerned without any English language corrections.

Box 2.4   Vocabulary of "A word in your ear" (Campbell, 1998)

The editor of "Nature" wrote the text cited in (Campbell, 1998). 20 words from the text (printed in blue) that may be unfamiliar are explained below. You may also be unaware of the identity of Ionesco mentioned in the text. He was a Romanian and French playwright who liked to make fun of ordinary situations and felt that much of life repeated itself without purpose.

dumbfounded – speechless with surprise
exasperate – annoy
convey – transmit
bestow – place a talent upon someone
overwhelm – overload with something
intricate – made with a complex design which is difficult to understand
sustain – keep going
ply – follow
considerable – significant or a large amount
bemoan – complain about
pore over – study *closely* and seriously
dismantle – take something apart
equation – an expression that *certain* quantities are equal to each other. They usually contain an equals sign (=). a + b = c is a basic equation.
tenure – have a permanent position, especially at a university
breed – a type or variety. This word is very important in genetics.
relish – look forward to and enjoy
nurture – look after and train
commendably – doing something in a way which deserves praise
conscientious – doing something very carefully
ineptness – inability

2.3   Take-home messages from Chapter 2

The take-home messages from this chapter are simply the eight headings from section 2.1. Write them down yourself without referring back to the chapter.

2.4 References

Articles
Campbell, P. (1998) A Word in Your Ear. Nature **394**, 403.
Carter-Siglow, J. (1997) Beyond the language barrier. Nature **384**, 509.
Hyland, K. and Jiang, F. (2017). Is academic writing becoming more informal?
    Engl. Specific Purp. **45**, 40–51.

Books
Bronowski, J. (1973) The Ascent of Man.
O'Toole, F. (2018) Heroic Failure.
Strunk, W., Jr. and White, E. B. (1918) The Elements of Style.

Websites
www.bartleby.com/141
www.pubmed.gov

2.5 Improvements to exercises

2.5.1 Improvements to box 2.1 "Shortening sentences by splitting them into two"

1. To be a good scientist, you have to be tolerant and patient when experiments or interpretations do not turn out as you had predicted. You must be able to stand high levels of frustration.
2. 62% of certified drug addicts believe that cannabis has *effects* on the behaviour of car drivers and machine operators which lengthen their reaction time. 45% of students shared this opinion whereas only 38% of customers interviewed at discotheques were aware of this negative effect of cannabis.
3. Finally, the correlation has been clearly shown. However, some *parameters remain* to be examined and further investigations should be done.
4. This results in texts which are extremely difficult to read. In addition, they also reveal to the world that their authors are clueless about paragraph structure.

2.5.2 Improvements to box 2.2 "Positive and negative sentences"

1. The experiment failed.
2. All *variables* tested remained constant.
3. This *hypothesis* lacks supporting evidence.
4. The variation was always less than 1%.
5. All alternative explanations seemed implausible.
6. Car drivers ignore both the fear of global warming and the number of fatal accidents.
7. This method is safe.
8. Everybody overlooked the *discrepancy* between the two sets of data.
9. The desired compound was absent from all the samples.
10. The mixture contained at least eleven substances.

2.5.3 Improvements to box 2.3 "Omit needless words!"

1. Figure 1 shows that the incidences of heart disease and television viewing *correlate* well.
2. 20% of the world population lacks clean water and sufficient food.
3. The effect of compound X on blood pressure remains to be determined.
4. Another important reason for this optimisation is to eliminate pollution.
5. Synergy will significantly reduce the amount of funding required.
6. Much work has *demonstrated* that the spherical Earth travels around the *similarly* shaped Sun.
Or: The Earth orbits the Sun.

> *I beg the reader only to remember that there is no language more difficult to write than English. No-one ever learns all that there is to be known about it. In the long history of our literature, it would have been difficult to find more than six persons who have written it faultlessly.*
> W. SOMERSET MAUGHAM

This chapter presents exercises to practise using the suggestions and guidelines of the first two chapters. Each of the three exercises is divided into two parts. The first part requires you to write your own text. The second part offers you the opportunity to improve texts written by former students. An improved *version* of each text *follows* directly for comparison.

3.1 Summarising the text "Fighting for Breath"

The first exercise is to summarise the article "Fighting for breath" in less than 200 words (box 3.1). Keep in mind that less than 200 words does not mean *exactly* 199 words. If only 50 words are necessary, then so much the better. In scientific writing, it is essential to be *able* to decide what is *relevant*. The sooner you begin to make such decisions, the more confident of your writing skills you will become.

The aim of the exercise is to learn how to omit needless words and build simple sentences to generate a condensed version. This cannot be achieved by taking entire sentences or phrases from the original text and trying to fit them together. That is plagiarism and must be avoided at all costs.

Here is a suggestion how to avoid plagiarism when making a summary. First, note down the *salient* facts of the original text on a piece of paper. Without looking at the original, use these notes to construct a hand-written draft of the summary. This should ensure that you use different sentence constructions to the original. Next, compare this first draft with the original article. If you find you have used words that were found in the original, use a thesaurus or dictionary to find alternatives. You can *confirm* that these words are absent from the original by searching the pdf file of the publication. If you cannot find an alternative word for a scientific or technical term, ensure that the sentence containing this term really is constructed in a different way.

Other *solutions* are, *of course*, possible. The most important thing is to be *aware* of avoiding plagiarism. If you practise expressing yourself in your own words, phrases and sentences, you will, with time, become adept and confident at this task.

In recent years, it has become possible to examine a text for plagiarism using on-line tools such as Grammaly's free plagiarism checker or the software iThenticate which involves a fee. If your university or institution has a subscription that allows you to use iThenticate, then I recommend you do so. As Editor-in-Chief of Archives of Virology, I use this regularly to examine submitted manuscripts and am always surprised how much plagiarism in manuscripts is detected by this software. In one incident, the software showed that much of a submitted manuscript had been taken from a previously published paper from the same group. Even the conclusions of the two texts were *identical*!

Finally, make sure that you read a printout of your work several times to *detect* typing errors, ensure that the sentences are linked together and omit needless words.

Box 3.1 Summarise the text "Fighting for breath"

Select the salient points in the article's 573 words and try to express them in less than 200 of your own. Jot down how many times you read and corrected your summary.

Fighting for breath

Dr Mark Porter highlights the *severe* threat to health posed
by air pollution and the need to take action.
(BBC Radio Times, 25th Sept. – 1st Oct. 1999, p. 38,
reprinted by permission)

The great fog of London in 1952 killed nearly 3,000 people in just four days according to this week's Secret History (Tuesday C4). Noxious smog as thick as pea soup may be a thing of the past but air pollution remains a major health issue that we ignore at our peril.

Traffic fumes are the biggest single *source* of pollutants. There are now some 24 million cars, 2.5 million vans, 450,000 trucks, 80,000 buses and 600,000 motorcycles on our roads (and a host of tractors and lawn mowers off them).

Total levels of the nastier types of vehicle emission have *decreased* since the introduction of catalytic converters in 1992, but are still too high for comfort.

There is now good evidence from across western Europe that high pollution levels lead to increased hospitalisation of people with chest problems such as asthma, particularly during *certain* atmospheric conditions – for example thunderstorms and long sunny periods (ultraviolet light acts on traffic fumes to produce ozone – a vital filter in the stratosphere but a highly irritant substance when breathed at ground level). The problem isn't confined to cities – ozone takes days to form, during which time it can drift. One of the highest readings taken in a recent ground-level ozone survey wasn't in London but in a pub car park in a Cotswold village near my home!

The relationship between air pollution and chest problems is complex. We *remain* unsure what effect it has on people with perfect lungs and there is no hard evidence that it is responsible for the dramatic rise in the incidence of asthma in the UK. We may have one of the highest rates of asthma in the world (at least one in ten children), but data from across the globe suggests there is no causal relationship. New Zealand has some of the cleanest air in the world but a high rate of asthma, and heavily polluted countries in eastern Europe have some of the lowest rates. Air pollution does worsen asthma (and hay fever for that matter), but it doesn't seem to *cause* it.

Staying indoors can be bad for your health, too. We spend around 90 per cent of our time indoors and recent studies suggest that air quality is worsening there, too, thanks to our modern airtight homes. The United States Environmental Protection Agency recently analysed samples of household dust and found levels of toxic heavy metals (such as lead and mercury) and pesticides that would mean the dust would be labelled hazardous waste if it was on the back of the truck! Other potentially dangerous pollutants discovered included the traffic pollutants carbon monoxide and nitrous oxide (from cooking and fires), and solvents from household products, including the cancer-causing tetrachloroethylene – *levels* of which sometimes exceeded World Health Organisation safe maximum limits for outdoors, let alone indoors.

The Government is trying to improve air quality but, as recent transport proposals have highlighted, it's a political minefield and an uphill struggle. It has also commissioned a survey of indoor pollution that is expected to result in new building regulations aimed at improving ventilation, but any benefits will be *limited* to newly built homes and offices. The real impetus for change must come from within – it's time we all shouldered the responsibility for the pollution we produce, both indoors and outdoors. Collective campaigns and legislation are all well and good, and much needed, but it's up to individuals to make them work.

Sections 3.2.1 to 3.2.4 present four summaries for improvement. How do they compare with yours? Do they have the same major points? Are they shorter or longer? How would you improve your summary? Like the four summaries here, yours probably has its good points, but it is also most *likely* in need of improvement. To see how, where and why the four summaries need attention, each has a set of specific comments and commands numbered in blue. The summaries were then modified to take these into account and generate the improved versions. Inserted text is in blue, deleted text has been removed.

The comments and commands numbered in blue were generated using the suggestions and questions for improving texts outlined in box 3.2. The specific suggestions and questions are applicable to almost every scientific text. You will notice that some of the remarks recur several times throughout the chapter. Section 3.7 lists the five most common ones. A similar list is found at the end of chapter 5 (section 5.7). The items in these two lists reflect the areas with which my students struggle the most and may therefore support you in identifying issues in your own work.

These comments are, however, not tablets of stone; they can be varied as can the order in which they are applied. What is important is that you question how a text is written and that you believe that every text has potential for improvement. Learn to attack a text, to look for chances to remove words, to call the meaning into doubt and to suggest other ways of expressing the thoughts. In writing, nobody is really wrong; there are just different points of view.

Brief examination of the four summaries *illustrates* the utility of the contents of box 3.2 for the identification of areas to improve. In the first summary (3.2.1), the paragraph construction is the major issue. Attending to the paragraph structure leads immediately to a solid summary with the major points. In the second (3.2.2), the paragraph construction is also at fault. *However,* the more *significant flaw* is that the summary has considerably exceeded the limit of 200 words. This one is therefore an opportunity to omit needless words. Summary 3 (3.2.3) has deficiencies in sentence construction as well as a *limited* vocabulary. Summary 4 (3.2.4) is very good as it stands, containing all the salient points. It only needs to be converted into formal English.

The students were supposed to use their own words as much as possible.

Did they? The author of the first summary made an excellent attempt. The efforts of authors 3 and 4 are acceptable. *In contrast*, the author of summary 2 could have made a greater *attempt* to find alternative words. This is one of the main *reasons* why the summary exceeds the limit of 200 words.

Learning to refine texts of others is one of the best ways of enhancing your own standard of writing. Clive James, the Australian television critic and author, provides support for this statement. In his autobiography, "Unreliable Memoirs", he states that he learnt his trade as a writer by correcting other people's work.

This section ends with my summary of "Fighting for Breath" (3.2.5) which contains just 57 words in three sentences. *Nevertheless*, it can certainly still be bettered. Can you suggest how to *strengthen* it?

Box 3.2   Identifying problems in written work

1. Read rapidly through a text to obtain an overview. Mark and correct spelling mistakes as well as expressions that are not formal. Underline sentences that require a linking word. Ask the questions "Does the text make sense?" and "Do I understand what is meant?" If not, mark these parts of the text. Are there large parts of the text that you do not understand? Then stop reading and discuss them, either in person or electronically, with the author.

2. If you feel that you understand the text, then read it slowly and carefully. Ask yourself the following questions:
Are all the paragraphs correct?
Are all the sentences straightforward and simple?
Do all the sentences make sense?
Do all the sentences fit together? Are they linked with the *correct* words?
Are there expressions that are repeated throughout the text?
Are there needless words?
Is it clear to which words pronouns such as "it", "they", "this" and "that" are referring?
Are adverbs placed close to the verbs that they qualify?

3. Start at the end and read the manuscript backwards, paragraph by paragraph. This ensures that the beginning and the end of the text are written in the same style. *Furthermore*, if the text has 40 pages, it is easy to run out of steam after reading page 20. *Consequently*, the second half will not be scrutinised as well as the first. Starting at the end avoids this little pitfall.

3.2.1 Summary 1 "Fighting for breath"

The article "Fighting for breath" is about air pollution, a great global problem nowadays (**1**).

It (**2**) based on the tragedy in London in 1952 where nearly 3.000 people were killed (**3**). Because (**4**) of a very noxious fog they were unalbe (**5**) to breathe (**1**).

"Fighting for breath" says that the different chest problems like asthma are not the reason (**6**) of traffic fumes and pollutants from cooking and fires. But (**4**) that facts (**7**) can worsen these illnesses rapidly. An example is New Zealand where is the cleanest air but nevertheless a high rate of asthma patients (**1, 3**).

So (**4, 8**) there must be another cause which lead to (**9**) chest problems. Dr Mark Porter, a radio speaker and a journalist, is sure that our airtight homes with lots (**10**) of toxic metals and pesticides are the reason (**6**) therefore (**11, 12**).

To protect our environment and ourselves (**8**) we should (**13**) limit indoor and outdoor pollution on the one hand and improve our home air quality on the other hand.

Word count: 155

Commentary. I am not sure about making paragraphs. Should there be an empty line between two paragraphs or not? Please correct me if necessary (**1**).

1 Paragraph construction is described in section 2.1.3. You must first decide what a paragraph is. Then you have two choices for the layout. You can show the start of a new paragraph by indenting the first line and show the end of the paragraph with the "enter" key (symbol ¶). This is the layout I always use. The second possibility is to leave an empty line between paragraphs and again show the end of the paragraph with the "enter" key. Whichever method you choose, do not use the "enter" key at the end of each sentence.

2 Part of the verb is missing.

3 The sentence construction is incorrect.

4 Avoid starting sentences with "and", "but", "because" or "so".

5 Switch your spellchecker on.

6 It is important to understand the difference between "reason" and "cause".

7 Always avoid this word. Replace it with a word referring to traffic fumes and pollutants.

8   Look at the use of commas, situation 3, in section 1.2.2.1.

8   Look at the use of commas, situation 3, in section 1.2.2.1. 8   Look at the use of commas, situation 3, in section 1.2.2.1.   8   Look at the use of commas, situation 3, in section 1.2.2.1. 8   Look at the use of commas, situation 3, in section 1.2.2.1.   8   Look at the use of commas, situation 3, in section 1.2.2.1.

8   Look at the use of commas, situation 3, in section 1.2.2.1.
9   Omit needless words.
10   Avoid "lots".
11   Does the article really say this?
12   Avoid ending sentences with "therefore".
13   A linking word is required.

Improved summary 1

The article "Fighting for breath" is about air pollution, a great global problem nowadays. It is based on the tragedy in London in 1952 in which nearly 3,000 people were killed. They were unable to breathe because of a very noxious fog. "Fighting for breath" says that the different chest problems like asthma are not caused by traffic fumes and pollutants from cooking and fires. However, these emissions can worsen these illnesses rapidly. An example is New Zealand which has very clean air but nevertheless a high rate of asthma patients. Thus, there must be another cause of chest problems. Dr Mark Porter, a radio speaker and a journalist, is sure that our airtight homes with high levels of toxic metals and pesticides are one of the causes.

To protect our environment and ourselves, we should, therefore, limit indoor and outdoor pollution on the one hand and improve our home air quality on the other hand.
Word count: 156

Dr Mark Porter writes in his article (**1**) "Fighting for breath" about the problems of our modern time (**1**) such as air pollution and diseases. (**2**) In 1952 (**3**) the Great Fog killed nearly 3000 people (**4**) caused by a combination of two high-pressure fronts creating a temperature inversion.

(**5**) The biggest (**6**) single source of pollutions are (**7**) the traffic fumes. Even the introduction of the catalytic converters in 1992 couldn't (**8**) solve the problem (**9**). This (**1**) environmental pollution is a factor in diseases like asthma, but the relationship between air pollution and chest problems is complex (**10**). Great Britain has one of the highest rates of asthma in the world, at least one in ten children! (**11, 12**) But (**13**) globally, there is no clear relationship. Because (**13**) New Zealand has some of the cleanest air in the world, but a high rate of asthma (**2, 14**).
(**2**) Another problem of the (**1**) traffic fumes is that they (**1**) produces (**7**) ozone. Not only cities are involved with this problem, also villages outside of the city (**1, 14, 15**).
One solution could be to stay inside for the whole day but it isn't! (**8, 12, 15**) Many people spend 90 per cent of their time indoors, but this could be bad for their health too (**16**). The (**17**) household dust includes (**18**) often toxic heavy metals (such as lead and mercury) (**19**) or pesticides. Carbon monoxide, nitrous oxide or cancer-causing tetrachlorethylene are only some examples (**16**).
It is fine (**20, 21**), that the population gradually gets to know (**1, 22**) about air pollution and his (**23**) risks. But (**13**) now it's (**8**) the time not only to speak about it (**1**) but also to live it (**20**).
Word count: 258

1   Omit needless words.
2   These sentences should be in the same paragraph.
3   Look at the use of commas, situation 3, in section 1.2.2.1.
4   This information is in the wrong place.
5   Is this a new paragraph or not? It does not fit with your paragraph formatting.
6   Avoid big in scientific writing. There are so many alternatives. Use a thesaurus to find them.
7   The subject and verb do not agree. Did you do a grammar check?

8 Always write out these forms.
9 Which problem do you mean? Be more specific.
10 Improve the structure of this sentence using a linking word.
11 Something is missing at the end of this sentence.
12 Avoid exclamation marks.
13 Avoid starting sentences with "and", "but", "because" or "so".
14 These are not complete sentences.
15 Make the sentence positive and clearer.
16 Delete this sentence. It contains unnecessary detail.
17 "The" should be deleted. "Household dust" is considered to be the same all over the world.
18 This word is used incorrectly.
19 Delete the text in the brackets. The information is not essential.
20 Find a more active word.
21 Look at the use of commas, situation 4, in section 1.2.2.1.
22 Avoid "get".
23 Use "its" to refer to things.

Improved summary 2

Dr Mark Porter writes in "Fighting for breath" about current problems such as air pollution and diseases. In 1952, the Great Fog, caused by a combination of two high-pressure fronts creating a temperature inversion, killed nearly 3,000 people.

The greatest single source of pollution is traffic fumes. Even the introduction of the catalytic converters in 1992 has not reduced their production. Environmental pollution is a factor in diseases like asthma; however, the relationship between air pollution and chest problems is complex. Great Britain has one of the highest rates of asthma in the world with at least one in ten children suffering. However, globally, there is no clear relationship. New Zealand has the cleanest air in the world, but also has a high rate of asthma. In addition, traffic fumes also produce ozone. Ozone *affects* both cities and the countryside.

One *solution* could be to stay inside for the whole day; *however, this* would be a mistake. Household dust often contains toxic heavy metals or pesticides.

It is important that the population *gradually* learns about air pollution and its risks. Now, it is time not only to speak but also to act.
Word count: 192

3.2.3 Summary 3 "Fighting for breath"

The article deals with air pollution in the UK which is to a large part (**1**) caused by traffic fumes, although the invention of catalytic converters brought a first amelioration (**2**).
Air pollution is still a major health issue, but the relationship between air pollution and health is complex. High pollution levels lead to increased hospitalization of people with chest problems. However (**3**) asthma incidence (**4**) is (**5**) not necessarily correlated with air pollution (**6**). Asthma (**7**) does not seem to be caused by air pollution (**6**), but worsened (**8**). *Additionally*, air pollution (**6**) also became (**9**) an indoor problem, (**10**) which is usually underestimated.
The government tries (**11**) to reduce air pollution by setting laws, but everyone is appealed upon (**12**) taking responsibility on his (**13**) own.
Word count: 114

1   Omit needless words.
2   This sentence is too complex.
3   Look at the use of commas, situation 3, in section 1.2.2.1.
4   Improve this expression.
5   This word is incorrect.
6   The expression "air pollution" occurs three times in quick succession. Find other words so that it occurs only once.
7   A linking word is missing.
8   Rewrite this sentence in the active form. Make sure that the cause is in the last part.
9   The tense is incorrect. Your sentence means that it is no longer a problem.
10 Improve the connection of "which" to "problem".
11 The tense is incorrect. Your sentence means that the government is not trying all the time. Or is that the meaning you want to express?
12 You have made an excellent attempt to use your own words. Unfortunately, this is not the right expression.
13 You should include the other half of the population.

The article deals with air pollution in the UK. This is mostly caused by traffic fumes, although the invention of catalytic converters brought a first amelioration.

Air pollution is still a major health issue, but the relationship between air pollution and health is complex. High pollution *levels* lead to increased hospitalization of people with chest problems. However, the incidence of asthma does not necessarily *correlate* with poor air quality. *Indeed, traffic fumes seem only to worsen asthma, but not to cause it.* Additionally, air pollution has also become an indoor problem, the extent of which is usually *underestimated*.

The government is trying to reduce air pollution by setting laws, but everyone is requested to take responsibility on his or her own.
Word count: 121

3.2.4 Summary 4 "Fighting for breath"

Air pollution, mainly caused by traffic fumes, is one of the major health issues in the UK. High pollution levels are discussed (**1**) to lead to chest problems, although the relationship is complex. But (**2**) also (**3**) air pollution indoors can lead to serious health problems. Recently (**4**) analysis of household dust found levels of toxic heavy metals and pesticides (**5**). Although the government is trying to improve air quality it's (**6**) up to the individuals to take action for a (**7**) healthier air (**8**).
Word count: 70

1   This word is incorrect.
2   Avoid starting sentences with "and", "but", "because" or "so".
3   Place "also" closer to the verb.
4   Look at the use of commas, situation 3, in section 1.2.2.1.
5   Something is missing.
6   Always write out these forms.
7   The "a" can be deleted. Healthier air is unique; there are not several different types. Look at guideline 3 in box 1.5.
8   Write this sentence more directly.

Air pollution, mainly caused by traffic fumes, is one of the major health issues in the UK. High pollution levels are thought to lead to chest problems, although the relationship is complex. However, air pollution indoors can also lead to serious health problems. Recently, *analysis* of household dust found *levels* of toxic heavy metals and pesticides above normal thresholds. The government *is trying* to improve air quality; nevertheless, it is up to everyone to take action for healthier air.

Word count: 79

3.2.5   Summary of "Fighting for breath" (Tim Skern)

Air pollution, both outdoor from traffic fumes and indoor from contaminated dust, significantly affects our health. Poor air containing UV-induced ozone has not been definitively shown to cause respiratory disease; however, it does appear to *worsen* ailments such as asthma. New governmental regulations may help, but the responsibility for improvement ultimately rests with us, the pollution producers.

Word count: 57, 3 sentences, read five times. Checked for own words.

Anything of importance can be said in 15 minutes.
LUDWIG WITTGENSTEIN

The first scientific text written by graduate students is usually an abstract of their *work* for a thesis committee or for a presentation at a scientific meeting. As they begin their writing, students usually ask "What is *actually* the difference between an abstract and a summary?" The answer is that there is essentially no difference. The Oxford English dictionary defines an abstract as a summary, especially of a scholarly piece of work. *Thus*, "abstract" is the word generally used by the scientific community for a summary.

Writing well-crafted abstracts is an important skill. For instance, imagine you are about to attend your first conference and wish to present your work. You will be asked for an abstract of your work when you register for the conference. The organisers will then use the abstract to select those participants who will give an oral presentation and those who will show a poster. Note that an oral presentation has the stronger impact. The organisers usually base their decision on the novelty of the work and the quality of the abstract. The writer of a concise and well-structured abstract has therefore a higher probability of being selected for an oral presentation. The abstract is even more decisive at some more exclusive meetings. Here, it may even determine who will be invited to attend and who can present *data*.

Practice in the writing of abstracts is, *therefore*, essential. An excellent exercise for this purpose is to write an abstract on your own work in just three sentences or less. I introduced this constraint into abstract writing after hearing a talk from Konrad P. Liessmann on Ludwig Wittgenstein. During the talk, Liessmann referred to the aphorism at the start of this section. For abstract writing, it can be rewritten as "Anything of importance can be summarised in three sentences."

Try this exercise now. It will force you to combine your writing skills with your understanding of your project. If you are an undergraduate without your own project, summarise a recent laboratory practical in three sentences. In the end, it does not really matter which theme you choose as long as you can condense it into just three sentences.

Students in my course are also requested to write a three sentence abstract. This forms an integral part of a ten minute oral presentation of their own work or of a publication from the scientific literature. At the end of the presentation, the audience discusses the quality, precision and *relevance* of the abstract as well as the use of English. In addition, the students receive ideas on how to improve their abstract.

Eight abstracts in need of strengthening are given in sections 3.4.1 to 3.4.8. Each is followed by an improved version. The first abstract is a fictitious *idea* for an exercise on body decoration used in my course. It comprises four sentences instead of three and is rather confused. *Nevertheless*, the comments and commands numbered in blue show that it can be rapidly shortened to three sentences without loss of information and that the abstract can be substantially clarified. The next six abstracts were part of an oral presentation based on the publications cited at the bottom of each abstract. All six abstracts can be rapidly improved by one round of editing using the guidelines in box 3.2.

There are a couple of points to mention about abstracts 7 and 8. You will notice that there is a second improved version of abstract 7 that was the product of a team discussion at a workshop that I held. You can see how much the abstract has benefitted from the discussion and how much has been changed from both the original version and the first improved version.

In contrast, abstract 8 is not from a presentation. Instead, it is a summary that a former student wrote about the cited article from Nature (Smil, 1999) on the importance of the Haber-Bosch process for human nutrition. I selected this summary for the third edition because it illustrates well how difficult it is for a non-native speaker to rewrite an article that has been already written in excellent English. Further, it contains two examples where it is unclear to which word a pronoun is referring. You can find the exercise itself and more about Vaclav Smil in section 8.4.

The number of comments and commands for each abstract may seem excessive, *considering* that each one is so short. One of the reasons for the number of comments is that writing abstracts can be very tricky. Often, students state that writing an abstract of a published paper was one of the most exacting tasks they had ever done. The reason is immediately apparent. The students had to take an entire publication, not just a short text like "Fighting for Breath", and rephrase it in three sentences without submitting to the temptation of taking phrases from the original abstract. Despite the difference in length between a publication and the text "Fighting for Breath", the technique for writing the abstract should still be the same. Put the publication away, note down the salient points, sketch the first draft with pen and paper and *search* for alternative words.

Look again at your own abstract. How many of the comments and commands would apply to yours? Why not give your abstract to your colleagues and see what comments they have? Use their comments to produce an improved version and file them for the future.

3.4.1 Abstract 1

The fashion of body decoration: risk of disease and psychological effects

Medical examinations and psychological surveys were done on different body decoration fashion (**1**) amongst people of young generation (**2**). Over 10000 were involved (**3**) in the examinations including blood tests for hepatitis C virus as well as psychological surveys (**4**). The *results* show a dependence of the rate (**5**) of positive hepatitis C virus infection (**2**) tests on the (**6**) age and on the time when (**7**) the body decorations were done. The psychological effects of body decoration vary with age (**4**).
Word count: 73

1 There are too many nouns in a row. In addition, the reason why you did the study should be clearer.
2 Omit needless words.
3 Include this information in the first sentence.
4 The abstract can be simplified and shortened to three sentences. First, describe the results of the medical examinations and then those of the psychological surveys.
5 A *rate* is a measure of the change of a quantity per unit time. It is therefore the wrong word in this sentence.
6 A word is missing.
7 Improve this expression.

The fashion of body decoration: risk of disease and psychological effects

Medical examinations and psychological surveys were done on 10,000 young people to determine the *differences* in and effects of body decoration. The examinations tested blood samples for hepatitis C virus; the results showed that the *probability* of a positive hepatitis C virus test depends on the person's age and the age at which the body decorations were done. The psychological surveys revealed that the effects of body decoration *vary* with age.
Word count: 71

3.4.2   Abstract 2

Arachnophobia

Arachnophobia is an abnormal and persistent fear of spiders which results in symptoms such as **(1)** feelings of panic, physiological and motor responses **(2)**. Swedish studies have shown **(3)** that probands **(4)** identified spiders on different **(1)** pictures faster **(5)** than harmless objects (mushrooms or flowers) **(6)**. Arachnophobics **(7)** detected the spiders even faster **(5)** than non-arachnophobics, so the fear of spiders enabled them to react more rapid **(8)**.
Word count: 59

Ohman *et al.* (2001) Emotion Drives Attention: Detecting the Snake in the Grass. J. Exp. Psychol. Gen. **130**, 466–478. (Abstract available through PubMed.)
Roach, J. (2001) Fear of Snakes, Spiders Rooted in Evolution, Study Finds.
http://news.nationalgeographic.com/news/2001/10/1004 _ snakefears.html

1   Omit needless words.
2   Improve the sentence construction.
3   You should first state the object of the study, not the result.
4   Proband is not used in this way in English. See box 3.3 for an explanation.
5   Use a better word or expression.
6   Remove the brackets.
7   Insert a linking word.
8   Improve the sentence construction and state the conclusion.

Arachnophobia

Arachnophobia is an abnormal and persistent fear of spiders which results in feelings of panic as well as causing physiological and motor responses. Swedish studies investigated whether trial subjects could identify spiders on pictures more rapidly than harmless objects such as mushrooms or flowers. Arachnophobics *indeed* detected the spiders even more quickly than non-arachnophobics did; thus, the authors *conclude* that the fear of spiders increased the speed of reaction of arachnophobics.

Word count: 71

3.4.3   Abstract 3

Acrylamide

Acrylamide is (**1**) a maybe (**2**) carcinogenic (**2**) substance (**1**), which (**1**) is used in the chemical industry and can be formed by (**3**) Maillard-reaction in food (**4**). A study, done in Switzerland (**1**), examined how the chemical content of the almonds and the temperature during preparation *affected* Acrylamide (**5**) formation in this foodstuff. A decreased (**6**) temperature for preparation (**7**) as well as employing almonds with modest *amounts* of unbound asparagine (**7**) enabled a *noteworthy decrease* (**6**) to be accomplished (**8**).

Word count: 67

Amrein *et al.* (2005) Acrylamide in Roasted Almonds and Hazelnuts. J. Agric. Food Chem. **53**, 7819–7825. (Abstract available *via* PubMed.)

1   Omit needless words.
2   Improve this word.
3   The definite article is required because the Maillard reaction is specified. Look at guideline 2 in box 1.5.
4   The sentence should be simplified.
5   Chemicals are not capitalised.
6   The word "decrease" appears twice in one sentence.
7   Look at the use of commas, situation 2, in section 1.2.2.1.
8   Simplify the sentence and make it more direct.

Acrylamide

Acrylamide, a *putative* carcinogen, is used in the chemical industry; it can also be formed by the Maillard-reaction in food. A Swiss study examined how the chemical content of the almonds and the temperature during preparation affected acrylamide formation in this foodstuff. A lower temperature for preparation, as well as employing almonds with modest amounts of unbound asparagine, clearly *decreased* the production of acrylamide.
Word count: 64

3.4.4   Abstract 4

Is DDT a justifiable weapon to fight malaria?

Dichlorodiphenyltrichloroethane (DDT) is a controversial weapon in the fight against malaria, one of the (**1**) serious public health problems in the world (**2**). Data (**1**) from the Pan-America Health Organization reveals that the (**1**) malaria cases clearly go down (**3**) when (**1**) house spraying (**3**) goes up (**3**). Enviromentalists (**4**) are concerned about DDT effects (**3**) on (**5**) environment and human health, it (**6**) is *however* the (**1**) potent weapon against the malaria mosquitoes (**3, 7**).
Word count: 61

Attaran *et al.* (2000) Balancing Risks on the Backs of the Poor. Nature Med. **6**, 729–730.
    (Article available *via* link through PubMed.)
https://sites.duke.edu/malaria/1-introduction-ddt-and-malaria/dilema/

1   One or more words are missing.
2   Omit needless words.
3   Improve this expression.
4   Switch on your spellchecker.
5   "The" is required before environment (only one) but not human health
        (all embracing).
6   It is not clear what "it" refers to.
7   Improve the sentence construction.

Is DDT a justifiable weapon to fight malaria?

Dichlorodiphenyltrichloroethane (DDT) is a controversial weapon in the fight against malaria, one of the most serious global public health problems. *Analysis* of data from the Pan-America Health Organization reveals that the number of malaria cases clearly *decreases* when the number of houses sprayed increases. Environmentalists are concerned about the *effects* of DDT on the environment and human health; however, DDT is still the most potent weapon against the mosquitoes carrying the malaria parasite.

Word count: 73

3.4.5 Abstract 5

An increase in measles reports [1] in the US are [2] causing concerns [3] for the HHS [4], the US Department of Health and Human Services. This significant [5] rise was primary [6] reported in a small community in Minnesota. Proceeded [7] investigations showed that the outbreak correlated with a decreasing number of [8] MMR vaccination, a shot that that immunizes [3] against measles, mumps and rubella [8].

Hall et al. (2017) Measles Outbreak – Minnesota April–May 2017. MMWR Morb. Mortal. Wkly Rep. 66, 713–717.

1 Make this clearer.
2 The subject and verb are not in agreement.
3 Omit needless words.
4 The abbreviation is unnecessary.
5 Only use significant if you have statistics.
6 The adjective is required.
7 Find a better word.
8 A word is missing.

Improved abstract 5

An increase in reports of measles in the US is a concern for the US Department of Health and Human Services. This appreciable rise was primarily reported in a small community in Minnesota. Subsequent investigations showed that the outbreak correlated with a decreasing number of people vaccinated against measles, mumps and rubella viruses.

3.4.6 Abstract 6

Plant-derived compounds stimulate the decomposition of organic matter in arctic permafrost soils

Arctic ecosystems are rapidly warming due to climate change, which promotes [1] the decomposition of soil organic matter. Furthermore, the [2] rising temperatures also [2] lead to an [2] increase in [2] plant productivity [3] and, as a consequence, to [2] an increased allocation of carbon and nitrogen containing [4] compounds (root litter, root exudates) [5] to the soil. These plant-derived organic compounds stimulate the soil organic carbon mineralization [6] and have the potential to [2] accelerate the ecosystem carbon losses [6] and amplify the positive feedback to global warming.

Wild et al (2016) Plant-derived compounds stimulate the decomposition of organic matter in arctic permafrost soils. Sci. Rep. **6** 25607

1 What is actually promoting decomposition?
2 Omit needless words.
3 Use a semi-colon to split the sentence in two halves
4 Use a hyphen to show to which word nitrogen and carbon belong
5 This is important information and should not be in brackets.
6 Simplify the expression

Improved abstract 6

Climate change is responsible for the rapid warming of Arctic ecosystems; this warming promotes the decomposition of soil organic matter. Furthermore, rising temperatures lead to increasing plant productivity; consequently, there is an increased allocation of carbon- and nitrogen-containing compounds from root litter and/or root exudates to the soil. These plant-derived organic compounds stimulate organic carbon mineralization in the soil and may accelerate carbon losses from the ecosystem and amplify the positive feedback to global warming.

The moss – a non-vascular plant in the fast lane

Air pollution, heavy metal pollution and contaminated water are examples for the legislating of humans [1]. By establishing industrialized countries [2], pollutants accumulated [3], and their dose became [4] detrimental for [5] ecosystems and our health, [6] wherefor [7, 8] some cities already use mosses to improve the air quality [9]. Lately [8], research showed [3] that F. hygrometrica is an important non-vascular plant for the adsorption [10] of heavy metals, such as lead [11].

Itouga et al. (2017) Protonema of the moss Funaria hygrometrica can function as a lead (Pb) adsorbent. PLoS ONE **12**: e0189726

1   This does not really make sense.
2   Is my suggestion below what you meant? Omit needless words to clarify.
3   The tense is incorrect.
4   Improve this expression.
5   The word is incorrect.
6   The sentence should end here.
7   Use your spellchecker.
8   Find a better word.
9   This sentence should be moved to the end.
10 Always be careful of the difference between adsorb and absorb.
11 Omit needless words

Improved abstract 7

Air pollution, heavy metal pollution and contaminated water are examples of human activity. Through industrialisation, pollutants have accumulated to such levels that they have become detrimental to ecosystems and our health. Recently, research has showed that *F. hygrometrica* is an important non-vascular plant for the adsorption of heavy metals. Indeed, some cities are already using mosses to improve the air quality.

Second version of improved abstract 7

Air and water pollution caused by heavy metal contamination are produced by human activity. Through industrialisation, concentrations of pollutants have become detrimental for ecosystems and human health; to improve air quality, certain cities are using mosses. Research has shown that the moss *F. hygrometrica* can adsorb heavy metals such as lead.

3.4.8   Abstract 8

Summary of "Detonator of the population explosion"
by Vaclav Smil

The article talks about [1] the discovery [2] and the great [3] impact of the Haber-Bosch process [4].

The process [5] is described as a synthetization [6] of ammonia, a substance that is highly needed [1] to produce inorganic nitrogen fertilizers. It [7] was *invented* by Frtiz Haber an [8] Carl Bosch. After documented setbacks [9] in 1909 [10] the [1] production was [1] started it [8] 1913. [4]

Until today [3], there is [11] an [12] utmost importance to the invention, as 130 million tonnes of ammonia are needed in agriculture each year [13]. These [7] could not be provided without the Haber-Bosch process [14], which would mean that [1] two fifths of the world's population could not be nourished [1, 15].
Smil, V. (1999) Detonator of the population explosion. Nature **400**, 415.

1 Omit needless words.
2 What is the difference between invention and discovery?
3 Find a better word.
4 Why is there a paragraph break here?
5 Word repetition. Link the two sentences together to overcome the issue.
6 "the synthesis" would have been clearer.
7 What does the pronoun refer to?
8 Read your work carefully.
9 Explain this in more detail.
10 Look at the use of commas, situation 3, in section 1.2.2.1.
11 Improve the sentence construction.
12 The article is incorrect.
13 Place these two words earlier in the sentence.
14 Use a semi-colon to split the sentence in two halves
15 Make the sentence positive.

The article discusses the invention and the tremendous impact of the Haber-Bosch process that enables the *synthesis* of ammonia, required to produce inorganic nitrogen fertilizers. Fritz Haber and Carl Bosch invented the process. Following the solution of certain documented problems in 1909, industrial production started in 1913. Even now, the invention is of utmost importance, as each year 130 million tonnes of ammonia are needed in agriculture. Such vast amounts could not be provided without the Haber-Bosch process; consequently, two fifths of the world's population would starve.

Box 3.3 Who takes part in a clinical study or trial?

In abstract 2, the author uses the word "proband" to *describe* someone taking part in a clinical study. In German, "proband" would be correct; in English, it is incorrect. The most apt word in English depends on the circumstances of the person taking part in the study. The possibilities include *"volunteer", "participant",* "test subject" and "trial subject". Note the subtle differences between them. The FDA (Food and Drug Administration) of the USA recommends "trial subject". If the trial subjects are ill, the word "patient" may also be used.

In scientific English, "proband" is used to describe members of a family who are being tested for the *presence* of a *particular* genetic trait. A paper on the genetic *background* of colour blindness on a Pacific island is an excellent example (Sundin *et al.*, 2000).

> *The most exciting phrase to hear in science, the one that heralds*
> *new discoveries, is not "Eureka!" ("I found it!")*
> *but rather, "Hmmm ... That's funny ..."*
> ISAAC ASIMOV

The third exercise in this chapter asks you to answer to the question "What is science?" Box 3.4 provides both a framework and some specific vocabulary to express your thoughts. To further stimulate your imagination, box 3.5 has eight texts from eminent scientists on various aspects of science. Whether they provide inspiration or not, the texts are full of useful scientific words. If you are still searching for more background on how science is done, the journal "Science" published an unusual article on how discoveries are made (Koshland, 2007).

You may think that the meaning or definition of science is purely academic. I disagree. In 2005, a judge in Pennsylvania gave a verdict instructing schools in the local district to *eliminate* all mention of intelligent design, supposedly an alternative to the *theory* of evolution, from school science courses. To arrive at his ruling, the judge first arrived at his own definition of science and then used this definition to *demonstrate* that intelligent design is not science (Mervis, 2006). This example highlights the importance of defining what science is and shows that the definition has a practical value. There are further references to the use of the definition of science to support the theory of evolution in the references to this chapter.

Box 3.4 "What is Science?" Answer this question in less than 300 words

Use at least three but not more than five paragraphs. Each paragraph should contain a set of ideas. Make sure that the sentences have a logical order and are linked together. Concentrate on writing short sentences that contain only one idea per sentence. The words below should not only be useful for this exercise but also serve to extend the basic list of words in box 1.7.

Questions
How?
How much?
What if?
Why?

Verbs
assume
diminish
elucidate
lessen
postulate
preclude
presume
reduce
reveal
speculate
visualise
wonder

Nouns
conjecture
conundrum
creativity
curiosity
enigma
fantasy
fortune
imagination
insight
invention
link
luck
paradigm
perception
postulate
prediction
proof
puzzle

rigour
serendipity
support
thought
truth
vision
wonder

Adjectives, adverbs
inquisitive
precise
repeatable
reproducible
specific
testable
valid
viable

Science cannot be divided into what is up to date and what is merely of anti-quarian interest; it is to be regarded as the product of a *growth* of thought.
Peter Medawar in "The Threat and the Glory: Reflections on Science and Scientists"

Science differs from other realms of human *endeavour* in that its substance does not derive from the activity of those who practise it.
Rosalind Franklin in a letter to Barry Commoner (quoted by Brenda Maddox in "Rosalind Franklin: The Dark Lady of DNA")

In science, as in other fields of endeavour, one finds saints and charlatans, warriors and monks, geniuses and cranks, tyrants and slaves, benefactors and misers ... Readers may suspect me of being in the pay of companies making agrochemicals, drugs, genes, or nuclear power plants, but I have no vested interest in any of these. My sole interest is in the survival of nature and of civili-sation.
Max F. Perutz in "Is Science Necessary?"

The task of the scientist is not just to see what nobody has yet seen. It is also to see what everybody has seen and to think what nobody has thought.
Arthur Schopenhauer

Late, very late, I discovered the true nature of science, of how it proceeds, of the men who do it. I came to understand that, contrary to what I had believed, the march of science does not consist in a series of inevitable conquests, or advance along the royal road of human reason, or result necessarily and *inevi-tably* from conclusive *observations* dictated by experiment and argumentation. I found in science a mode of playfulness and imagination, of obsessions and fixed ideas. To my surprise, those who achieved the unexpected and *invented* the possible were not simply men of learning and method. More than anything else, they possessed extraordinary minds, enjoyed the difficult, and often were creatures of amazing vision. Those in the front ranks displayed exotic blends of passion and indifference, of rigor and whimsy, naïveté, and the will to power, in a triumph of individuality.
Starting to work in Andre Lwoff's laboratory at the Pasteur Institute, I found myself in an unfamiliar universe of limitless *imagination* and endless criticism. The game was that of continually *inventing* a possible world, or a piece of possi-ble world, and then of comparing it with the real world. Doing experiments was to give free rein to every *idea* that crossed my mind ...
Francois Jacob in "The Statue Within: An Autobiography"

Hypothesis formation is an exercise in the use of the imagination to *explain* data and to make predictions.

Baruch S. Blumberg in his autobiography "Hepatitis B: The Hunt for a Killer Virus"

I have never done anything "useful". No *discovery* of mine has made, or is *likely* to make, directly or indirectly, for good or ill, the least difference to the amenity of the world. I have helped to train other mathematicians, but mathematicians as the same kind as myself, and their *work* has been, so far at any rate as I have helped them to it, as useless as my own. Judged by all practical standards, the value of my mathematical life is nil; and outside mathematics it is trivial anyhow. I have just one *chance* of escaping a verdict of complete triviality, that I may be judged to have created something worth creating. And that I have created something is undeniable: the question is about its value.

The case for my life, then, or for that of any one else who has been a mathematician in the same sense in which I have been one, is this: that I have added something to knowledge, and helped others to add more; and that these somethings have a value which differs in degree only, and not in kind, from that of the creations of the great mathematicians, or of any of the other artists, great or small, who have left some kind of memorial behind them.

G. H. Hardy in "A Mathematician's Apology"

Tim Skern comments: I have to disagree most strongly with you, Mr. Hardy. The Hardy-Weinberg *equilibrium* (Hardy, 1908; Weinberg, 1908) was and still is extremely useful. One hundred years after its formulation, geneticists continue to make use of it.

I just like to know why things happen and I think that is probably something we have inherited. Curiosity about things, why things happen, can prepare you for how you live in the world. It has great survival value, this sort of curiosity, and it is a question of how your curiosity is directed. Many people are very curious about things, are obsessed about things, which you could say have no *consequence*.

James Watson answering the question "Why do scientists do science?" in the book "On Giants' Shoulders" by Melvin Bragg.

Students' texts on "What is science?" generally cover a range of opinions, depending on the *backgrounds* of the students, their maturity and their fields of study. The four (3.6.1 to 3.6.4) chosen for this section are all excellent examples. All are creative and stimulating, but, *of course*, all need work. Most of the comments and commands again focus on formal English and writing technique. One comment, on the misuse of the words "prove" or "disprove", is found in the comments on the first three texts. Box 3.6 explains in detail the background to the meaning and proper use of these two words.

Look at the improved versions and examine *closely* the modifications. This single round of improvement has greatly smoothed them over. Nevertheless, all of them still *require* a second round. Use the guidelines in box 3.2 to identify parts to be strengthened and decide on the changes you would make next.

This chapter was designed not only to develop your writing technique, but also to stimulate you to ponder important questions of our time and to reflect on the nature of science itself.

Box 3.6   Using the words "prove" and "disprove"

"Prove" is an interesting word. In former times, it meant "to test" as in the sentence "The exception *proves* (i.e. *tests*) the rule." Over time, it has evolved to mean nowadays "demonstrating something with certainty".

This explanation *illustrates* why "prove" and "*disprove*" should not be used with the word "hypothesis". Scientists put forward a hypothesis (or an idea or a conjecture or a postulate) to answer a *question* or tackle a problem. They then set out to test the hypothesis. They look for evidence in support of the hypothesis or *evidence* indicating that the *hypothesis* is false. They do not set out to prove or disprove a hypothesis.

If a hypothesis holds true for a large number of *observations* or measurements, it may develop into a theory (*for example,* Darwin's theory of evolution or Einstein's theory of relativity). If the theory turns out always to be true, it may be called a law (for instance, Mendel's laws of heredity or the laws of thermodynamics). "Prove" and "disprove" can be used for a theory or a law.

3.6.1 Text 1 "What is science?"

There are (**1**) many subjects, which (**1**) have been given the attribute "scientific". Several of this (**2**) "sciences" are working together on a problem,
while others are competing in their opinions. To answer the question
after (**1**) the general characteristics of science, it is necessary to define
what all scientific fields have in common.
Lexica tell us that science is the entirety of knowledge, referring to one
subject, which is put in a logical relation by the methodological process
of interdisciplinary reproducible research and cognition to find reality
(**3**).[1]
A scientist is then someone who is aiming (**4**) to *increase* the knowledge
within his (**5**) research field. He/She (**6**) does this by developing mental
or physical experiments based on his/her (**6**) hypothesis. The later (**7**)
are themselves made from logical deduction of already (**1**) existing and
proven theories. By proving (**8**) his/her ideas (**6**), the scientist is able to
define increasingly the limits of probability, (**9**) that a certain phenomena
(**10**) happens (**11**).
Nonetheless (**12**) every scientist has to find out, (**9**) that there will never
be absolute security (**13**), randomness will always play a role, too (**14**).
There is a science even about this randomness which tries to specify it
and to keep it within certain limits.
So (**12, 15**) all in all (**1**) science is the dream of understanding a real world,
(**9**) that is in itself not existing (**16**), because it unexceptionally (**13**)
depends on the *perspective* of the observer and can, therefore, never be
absolutely certain and objective (**17**).
Word count: 226

1 Translated from Brockhaus

1 Omit needless words.
2 Did you read your work?
3 This direct quote should be in quotation marks.
4 The tense is incorrect.
5 You should include the other half of the population.
6 Avoid writing he/she or his/her in these sentences.
7 This word fooled your spellchecker. *Consequently*, the whole paragraph
became difficult to understand.
8 Use "prove" only for theories and laws. See box 3.6 for further information.

9   Look at the use of commas, situation 4, in section 1.2.2.1.

10   The singular of this word is required here.

11   The construction of this sentence is poor.

12   Look at the use of commas, situation 3, in section 1.2.2.1.

13   Find a better word.

14   Avoid ending a sentence with "too".

15   Avoid starting sentences with "and", "but", "because" or "so".

16   The construction of the negative is incorrect.

17   This sentence is too long and complex.

Improved text 1

Many subjects have been given the attribute "scientific". Several of these "sciences" are *working* together on a problem while others are competing in their opinions. To summarise the general characteristics of science, it is necessary to define what all scientific fields have in common.

Lexica tell us that "science is the entirety of knowledge, referring to one subject, which is put in a logical relation by the methodological process of interdisciplinary reproducible *research* and cognition to *find* reality."[1]

A scientist is then someone who aims to increase the knowledge within his or her research field. Scientists do this by developing mental or physical experiments based on their hypotheses. The latter are themselves made from logical deduction of existing and proven theories. By testing their ideas, scientists are able to define increasingly the limits of probability and *predict* whether a certain phenomenon will happen.

Nonetheless, every scientist has to find out that there will never be *absolute* certainty; in addition, randomness will always play a *role*. There is a science even about this randomness which tries to specify it and to keep it within certain limits.

Thus, science is the dream of understanding a real world that in itself does not exist, because it absolutely depends on the perspective of the observer. Science can, therefore, never be absolutely certain and objective.

Word count: 220

1   Translated from Brockhaus

Once upon a time there was curiosity. That was the time when the fairy tale of science started. I call it (**1**) fairy tale because science is a never-ending story.

At the beginning of any scientific work, there is always a question. Often (**2**) this question is related to a problem of every day life. In former days (**2**) scientists solved a lot of (**3**) difficult problems, like diseases (**4**). During (**5**) the years (**2**) our life standard (**6**) increased (**7**), because of (**8**) the interventions (**5**) scientists made in the past (**9**).

Another motivation for science is often a discovery. Something interesting we observed, for example, in the (**10**) nature (**11**). We are curious about it and want to find an explanation for it.

(**12**) Scientific work is a puzzle of *assumptions*, imagination, inference and vision. It happens that (**9**) someone disproves (**13**) a hypothesis and shows that the *insight* the first scientist had was wrong. This is also a part of science; to learn to live with disappointments (**14**). A scientist should never give up and should be able to try experiments again and again. From this (**2**) it is becomes clear that science is a never-ending fairy tale. Word count: 182

1 There is an article missing. Look at guideline 1 in box 1.5.
2 Look at the use of commas, situation 3, in section 1.2.2.1.
3 Avoid "a lot".
4 Some words are missing.
5 This word is incorrect.
6 This expression is incorrect.
7 The tense is incorrect. Your sentence means that it is no longer increasing.
8 This expression can be improved.
9 Omit needless words.
10 This article should be omitted. Look at guideline 3 in box 1.5.
11 This not a complete sentence. Add the information to the previous sentence.
12 Is this a new paragraph or not? It does not fit with your paragraph formatting.
13 Use "disprove" for a law or theory. Find a better word. See box 3.6 for further details.
14 The second part of the sentence is lacking a verb and is therefore not a complete sentence. Insert a suitable verb.

Once upon a time there was curiosity. That was the time when the fairy tale of science started. I call it a fairy tale because science is a never-ending story.

At the beginning of any scientific work, there is always a question. Often, this question is related to a problem of everyday life. In former days, scientists *solved* many difficult problems such as treating diseases. Over the years, our standard of living has increased due to the inventions of scientists.

Another motivation for science is often a *discovery,* something interesting we observed, for example, in nature. We are curious about it and want to find an explanation for it.

Scientific *work* is a puzzle of assumptions, imagination, inference and vision. *Occasionally,* someone falsifies a hypothesis and shows that the insight the first scientist had was wrong. This is also a part of science; one must learn to live with disappointments. A scientist should never give up and should be able to *try* experiments again and again.

From this, it is becomes clear that science is a never-ending fairy tale.

Word count: 177

I think curiosity and the desire to understand the processes of life are characteristic to human beings. Over thousands of years, mankind has found different ways like (**1**) magic, religion or science to *explain* the phenomena of nature.

The difference between scientific theories and other approaches is that science is based on the existence (**1**) of evidence. The first step in research is to collect (**1**) hypotheses. By observation (**2**) the scientist *gains* insight and forms a theory. In an experiment with defines (**3**) parameters (**2**) the outcome can be measured and ideas can be either proved or disproved (**4**). Nevertheless (**2**) it's (**5**) difficult to deduce (**1**) from artificially created scenarios to universal laws, especially in natural science. In nature (**2**) a lot (**6**) of variabilities (**1**) exist, e. g. (**7**) no human being equals another – (**8**) and those differences can't (**5**) be included in experiments (**9**).

At the beginning of science (**2**) the motives for research were curiosity, imagination and to strive (**10**) for knowledge. A lot (**6**) of milestones, such as the discovery of Penicillin (**11**) by Alexander Fleming, were serendip-ity (**12**). Nowadays (**2**) science is of economic importance and has a great influence on our everyday life. Medicine, transport and communica-tion – (**8**) everything is based on the latest state of knowledge, gained by researchers all over the world.

A lot (**6**) has changed since the first scientist started to ask questions, *speculated* and developed presumptions. Nevertheless, (**13**) the basic motivation of science – (**8**) human curiosity – (**8**) and the complexity of nature will always lead to new questions.

Word count: 231

1   Find a better word or expression.
2   Look at the use of commas, situation 3, in section 1.2.2.1.
3   Did you read your work?
4   Do not use "proved" or "disproved" for ideas. See box 3.6 for
    further information.
5   Always write out these forms.
6   Avoid "a lot".
7   Avoid using abbreviations as part of the sentence.
8   Avoid the dash.
9   The structure of this sentence is poor.

10 The sentence structure is inconsistent.

11 Chemicals are not capitalised.

12 An adjective is required here.

13 Some words are missing.

Improved text 3

I think curiosity and the desire to understand the processes of life are characteristic to human beings. Over thousands of years, mankind has found different ways such as magic, religion or science to explain the phenomena of nature.

The *difference* between scientific theories and other approaches is that science is based on the generation of evidence. The first step in research is to put forward hypotheses. By observation, the scientist gains insight and forms a *theory*. In an experiment with defined *parameters*, the outcome can be measured and ideas can be verified or falsified. Nevertheless, it is difficult to proceed from artificially created scenarios to universal laws, especially in natural science. In nature, much *variation* exists; for instance, no human being equals another. Such differences cannot be included in experiments.

At the beginning of science, the motives for *research* were curiosity, imagination and the search for knowledge. Many milestones, such as the *discovery* of penicillin by Alexander Fleming, were serendipitous. Nowadays, science is of economic importance and has a great influence on our everyday life. Medicine, transport and communication are all based on the latest state of knowledge, gained by researchers all over the world.

Much has changed since the first scientist started to ask questions, speculated and developed presumptions. Nevertheless, the combination of the basic motivation of science, human curiosity, and the complexity of nature will always lead to new questions.

Word count: 232

3.6.4 Text 4 "What is science?"

Firstly, I would like to present my own general definition of science. Science is the human activity in the field between (**1**) known and (**1**) unknown. The border which divides these areas is not precise. A scientist should possess high intelligence and intuition to balance between them (**2**). The turn over the unknown moves to (**3**) an unstable world of illusions. On the other hand, a natural desire to stay in the safe area of the known may results (**4**) in primitive scientific researches (**5**).

I have found my favourite definition of science in Pushkin's poetry:

> Experience that is a result of difficult mistakes,
> a genius who is a friend of paradoxes,
> the spirit of education
> prepare many wonderful discoveries.

The origin (**6**) is very beautiful. One day (**7**) when my English will be (**8**) good enough (**7**) I will try again to translate it. This is a very short but excellent example of a definition including the main attributes of the object: (**9**) the specificity of scientific activity, the type of person which (**10**) should have (**2**) deals with science and desirable results. Certainly, it is a definition of idealistic science. But (**11**) it is very important to have such ideals in the mind to make scientific work more interesting and, maybe (**12**), more productive.

Word count: 201

1   You need the definite article here because the "known" and "unknown" are assumed to be defined and therefore specific.
2   Omit needless words.
3   This sentence is unclear. My solution is guesswork.
4   Did you read your work?
5   Research is generally singular.
6   I think you mean "original". Note the difference between the two words.
7   Look at the use of commas, situation 2, in section 1.2.2.1.
8   The tense is incorrect.
9   The colon is used incorrectly. Two complete thoughts are being separated. A full-stop is therefore required. See section 1.2.2.3 for the use of colons.
10 Use "who" when referring to people.
11 Avoid starting sentences with "and", "but", "because" or "so".
12 Find a better word.

Firstly, I would like to present my own general definition of science. Science is the human activity in the field between the known and the unknown. The border which divides these areas is not precise. A scientist should possess high intelligence and intuition to balance them. Entering into the unknown takes us to an unstable world of illusions. On the other hand, a natural desire to stay in the safe area of the known may result in primitive scientific research.

I have found my favourite definition of science in Pushkin's poetry:

Experience that is a *result* of difficult mistakes,
a genius who is a friend of *paradoxes*,
the spirit of education
prepare many wonderful discoveries.

The original is very beautiful. One day, when my English is good enough, I will try again to translate it. This is a very short but excellent example of a definition including the main attributes of the object. These include the *specificity* of scientific activity, the type of person who should deal with science and desirable results. Certainly, it is a definition of idealistic science. However, it is very important to have such ideals in the mind to make scientific work more interesting and, perhaps, more productive.
Word count: 202

3.7   The five most common commands and comments from improved texts in Chapter 3

Here are the five most frequent commands and comments I made to the students' texts in this chapter. To simplify matters, I counted similar comments (e.g. "improve this word" and "improve this expression") as the same. Keep these five comments in mind when redacting your own work.

▌ A word or expression is missing or the present one needs improving.
▌ The sentence structure needs improving or the sentence is too complex.
▌ Omit needless words
▌ Look at the use of commas, situation 3, in section 1.2.2.1
▌ A linking word is required.

▌ Summarise texts and write abstracts in your own words and sentences.
▌ Never cut and paste other people's work.
▌ Be decisive in selecting the salient points.
▌ Every text can be improved.
▌ Think about your writing. What might an uninitiated reader think?
▌ Ask specific questions to identify sentences or paragraphs needing work.
▌ Call every word, sentence and paragraph into question.
▌ Be aggressive in omitting needless words.
▌ Read your own texts critically before giving them to someone else.
▌ Respect other people's comments and criticisms.

3.9   References

Articles

Amrein, T. M., Lukac, H., Andres, L., Perren, R., Escher, F. and Amadò, R. (2005) Acrylamide in Roasted Almonds and Hazelnuts. J. Agric. Food Chem. **53**, 7819–7825.

Attaran, A., Roberts, D. R., Curtis, C. F. and Kilama, W. L. (2000) Balancing Risks on the Backs of the Poor. Nature Med. **6**, 729–730.

Hall V, Banerjee E, Kenyon C, *et al.* (2017) Measles Outbreak – Minnesota April–May 2017. MMWR Morb. Mortal. Wkly Rep. **66**, 713–717.

Hardy, G. H. (1908) Mendelian Proportions in a Mixed Population. Science **28**, 49–50.

Itouga, M., Hayatsu, M, Sato, M., Tsuboi, Y., Kato, Y., Toyooka, K. et al. (2017) Protonema of the moss Funaria hygrometrica can function as a lead (Pb) adsorbent. PLoS ONE 12(12): e0189726.

Koshland, D. E. (2007) The Cha-Cha-Cha Theory of Discovery. Science **317**, 761–762.

Mervis, J. (2006) Judge Jones Defines Science – and Why Intelligent Design isn't. Science **311**, 34.

Ohman, A., Flykt, A. and Esteves, F. (2001) Emotion Drives Attention: Detecting the Snake in the Grass. J. Exp. Psychol. Gen. **130**, 466–478.

Porter, M. (1999) Fighting for Breath. BBC Radio Times 25th Sept.–1st Oct. 1999, 38.

Smil, V. (1999) Detonator of the population explosion. Nature **400**, 415.

Sundin, O. H., Yang, J. M., Li, Y., Zhu, D., Hurd, J. N., Mitchell, T. N., Silva, E. D. and Maumenee, I. H. (2000) Genetic Basis of Total Colourblindness among the Pingelapese Islanders. Nature Genet. **25**, 290–293.

Voosen, P. (2018) The realist. Science, **359**, 1320–132

Weinberg, W. (1908) Über den Nachweis der Vererbung beim Menschen. Jahresh. Verein f. vaterl. Naturk. Württem. **64**, 368–382.

Wild, B., Gentsch, N., Capek, R. *et al* (2016) Plant-derived compounds stimulate the decomposition of organic matter in arctic permafrost soils. Sci. Rep. **6**, 25607

Books

Bragg, M. (1998) On Giants' Shoulders: Great Scientists and their Discoveries from Archimedes to DNA.

Blumberg, B. S. (2002) Hepatitis B: The Hunt for a Killer Virus.

Hardy, G. H. (1940) A Mathematician's Apology.

Jacob, F. and Philip, F. (1987) The Statue Within: An Autobiography.

James, C. (1981) Unreliable Memoirs.

Maddox, B. (2002) Rosalind Franklin: The Dark Lady of DNA.

Medawar, P. B. (ed. Pyke, D.) (1990) The Threat and the Glory: Reflections on Science and Scientists.

Maugham, W. S. (1930) The Gentleman in the Parlour.

Perutz, M. F. (1989) Is Science Necessary?

Websites

Duke University. DDT and Malaria.
https://sites.duke.edu/malaria/1-introduction-ddt-and-malaria/dilema/

Matzke, N. (2009) The Testimony of Kevin Padian in *Kitzmiller* v. *Dover*.
https://ncse.com/creationism/legal/padians-expert-testimony

Roach, J. (2001) Fear of Snakes, Spiders Rooted in Evolution, Study Finds.
http://news.nationalgeographic.com/news/2001/10/1004_snakefears.html

www.nap.edu/sec

www.grammarly.com/plagiarism-checker

www.ithenticate.com

> *Gradually the sheer weight of negative evidence began to*
> *convince me that writing is essentially a matter of saying*
> *things in the right order.*
> CLIVE JAMES

Constructing a scientific manuscript is a challenge. It does not matter whether an author is writing a manuscript for the first or for the hundredth time. It is hard work to ensure that an anonymous reader, whom you have never met and who may be unfamiliar with your work, will have a *chance* to comprehend your scientific writing. You must, among other things, *attempt* to *clarify* your ideas, simplify your sentences, omit needless words, improve the quality of the figures containing the data and attend to all the other important details *necessary* for scientific accuracy. The effort required to carry out all these tasks should not be underestimated.

The goal of chapter 4 is to help reduce the effort required to construct a scientific manuscript. There are suggestions on how to write each of the sections and, at the end of the chapter, on how to improve the first draft. If you keep these suggestions in mind, you should need less effort to produce a better quality manuscript. The improvement in quality will be reflected in a higher probability of rapid publication; the reduced effort will be visible in smaller piles of paper.

4.1   The process of publishing original data in a scientific manuscript

Undergraduates and young postgraduate students are often unclear about the general process of publishing data in a scientific journal. This section aims to provide the background to make the process more transparent. Box 4.1 outlines the most common steps in scientific publication as well as the connections between them. The first step, the choice of journal, is crucial as it defines how you will write your manuscript. Your supervisor or the senior scientist in your laboratory will usually assist you in selecting the most suitable one. The final decision will depend, amongst other things, on the theme and novelty of your work as well as the amount of data you wish to publish. You can start the selection process by browsing through journals which you think may be candidates and generating an initial short list. Browsing the journals will also start to prepare you for writing the manuscript. You will acquire a feeling for the style of the journals, the arrangement of the sections, the style of the articles and how much data is usually to be found. For clarity, be *aware* that scientists refer to written work before acceptance for publication as a manuscript. After publication, scientists refer to the published work as a publication, an article or a paper.

The choice of journal for submission of your manuscript is nowadays also heavily influenced by the so-called impact factor of the journal. Your supervisor may ask you to find out the impact factors of the journals on your short list. He or she may be *trying* to *increase* the number of impact factors collected per year as this is a common, if controversial, method of evaluating scientific *output*. The impact factor of a scientist may count towards promotion, an award for more equipment from a university or funding from agencies that *support* scientific work. Box 4.2 provides more information on impact factors and their calculation.

Once you have chosen your journal, you can start to write the manuscript, proceeding through the straightforward steps two to four in box 4.1. In step five, the manuscript is submitted to the journal and now enters the hands of the journal's editor. The subsequent steps six and seven, the *role* of the editor and peer review, are at the heart of the *process* of publishing scientific data. They are also the two steps about which most young scientists have questions. How does someone become an editor? What does an editor do? What is peer review and how does it *work*?

Let us answer these questions one by one. Editors of journals are usually chosen by the publishers of journals for their scientific standing. An editor's reputation should guarantee the scientific quality and integrity of a journal and attract manuscript submissions. The first thing an editor does on receiving a manuscript is to examine whether it falls within the scope of the journal. If this is the case, the editor will send the manuscript out for peer review.

Peer review is the name given to the anonymous evaluation process which is almost universally employed to gauge the suitability of a manuscript for publication. Peers in the language of science are respected members of the community who have published extensively in a *particular* field. Editors select them because they can be expected to review and judge the quality, novelty and significance of new research findings in a manuscript submitted for publication. The peers (usually two, sometimes three, per manuscript) will write reports on the above mentioned issues as well as on any other points they find *relevant*. The reports will also include comments on the overall suitability of the manuscript as well as a formal recommendation whether it should be accepted, modified or rejected. The editor makes the final decision based on these reports. If the reviewers' reports differ substantially, the editor may review the manuscript or ask another peer to examine and comment on the manuscript in the light of the first two reviewer's comments. *Additionally,* the editor should ensure that the reviews are fair and discard any that are unsubstantiated or appear to have been motivated by spite or rivalry.

How long does peer review take? You can find this parameter quite easily as published manuscripts usually state on the first page when a manuscript was received for review and when it was accepted. Generally, the process takes more than one month but may take much longer. Why should this be so when many journals state on their web pages that reviewers are asked to complete their reviews within 14 days? As reviewers generally perform this task without a fee, it is not surprising that they often require more days for completion. Further, a conscientious reviewer may also need more time to suggest constructively how a manuscript can be improved so that is acceptable for publication. Manuscripts that describe breakthroughs in the field or which challenge current dogma or paradigms may also take longer for the peer review process to be completed. More days will also be needed if the initial reviewers fail to agree on the quality of a manuscript, so that a third reviewer is subsequently invited to resolve the discrepancy.

Very occasionally, you will observe that a manuscript was accepted for publication just a few days after receipt. There may of course be a simple explanation for the rapid acceptance of a manuscript. For instance, some journals reject manuscripts that require major revision and require that they are resubmitted as a new manuscript. If the authors have carried out the revision to the editor's satisfaction, then she or he may accept the manuscript without any review. On the other hand, a rapid acceptance may mean that the peer review process has not been carried out thoroughly. The article by Adams et al (2009) was accepted after just two days by the Journal of Biological Chemistry. Look at the axes in figures 1 and 4 and decide for yourself how intense the peer review of this paper was.

The editor and the reviewers will have a special relationship to your manuscript, as they will be the first people outside your circle of co-authors, colleagues and friends to read it. When you are writing, try to imagine how the editor and reviewer might find your manuscript. Bear in mind that editors and reviewers are busy people who often receive little or no payment for their time and trouble. Anything that saves their time, such as a clearly written and logically constructed manuscript, will make them feel well-disposed to your work. Anything that wastes their time, even something as trivial as a manuscript without page numbers, will annoy them and your manuscript may consequently suffer.

Nowadays, peer review is not restricted to manuscripts. Almost everything in science today is submitted for peer review, whether it be a proposal to a funding agency for support for a scientific project or an *application* for a fellowship for post-doctoral work. It is also quite possible nowadays that your Ph. D. thesis will be subject to peer review. If your thesis is to be *judged* by an *external* examiner, it is vital that you put yourself in the position of the reviewer and ask yourself how she or he will find your *work*. A reviewer who has to evaluate 200 pages of *inaccurate* and confused writing is unlikely to give high marks.

Returning again to the steps outlined in box 4.1, we have seen that reviewers can recommend that the editor accepts a manuscript, either as it is or after modification, or rejects it. Manuscripts accepted without change are a rare occurrence. It is more usual for the reviewers to recommend some degree of revision. Occasionally, the requested revisions are only minor corrections and typographical errors. More often, the reviewers require substantial changes including more detailed explanations, additional experiments or controls. Such requests for further data can be annoying, but the reviewers' recommendations almost always lead in the end to an improved piece of work. It is difficult to accept sometimes, but you should try to keep this in mind when reading the reviewers' *reports*.

Reviewers can, however, recommend that a manuscript is unsuitable for publication and that it should be returned to the authors. A manuscript can be rejected, as it is generally termed, for several *reasons. For instance*, the content may not be suitable for the particular journal, the scientific results may not represent a sufficiently large advance in knowledge or the quality of the *data* is perhaps poor. Reviewers may reject a manuscript because the results do not justify the conclusions or because the significance of the results has been misinterpreted or over-interpreted.

It is rare, though, that a manuscript is rejected simply because it is *poorly* written. Reviewers are *primarily* concerned with the science contained within a manuscript. If the scientific quality is poor, the reviewers will recommend rejection, regardless of how well written the manuscript is. If the quality of the science is acceptable, they turn to the quality of the writing. If this is not acceptable, they will suggest to the editor that the authors improve the writing and submit a revised *version*.

This chapter began by stating that constructing a scientific manuscript is a challenge. Let us now take up this challenge and construct a manuscript that would have the best possible *chance* of a positive passage through the peer review process.

Box 4.1   The steps in constructing and publishing a scientific manuscript

1. Choose a suitable journal.
2. Write, read and improve the manuscript.
3. Give the complete manuscript to friends or colleagues and ask them to read it critically.
4. Examine their comments, criticisms and suggestions and modify the manuscript *accordingly*. Read the manuscript again with great care.
5. Submit the manuscript using the chosen journal's on-line submission software.
6. The editor of the journal sends the manuscript out for peer review.
7. The reviewers find the manuscript:

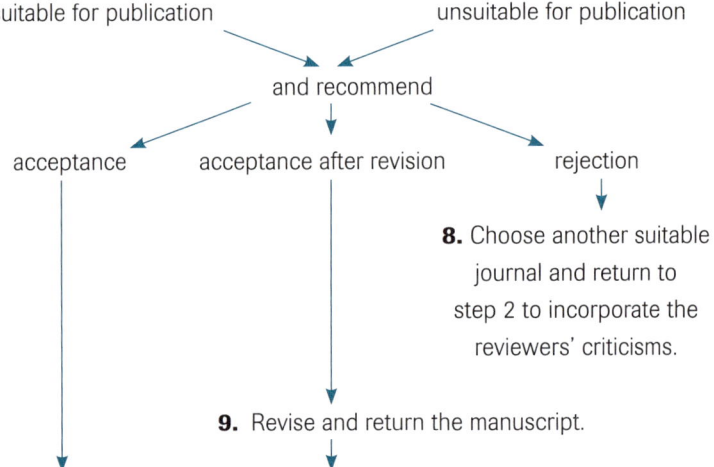

suitable for publication   unsuitable for publication

and recommend

acceptance   acceptance after revision   rejection

8. Choose another suitable journal and return to step 2 to incorporate the reviewers' criticisms.

9. Revise and return the manuscript.

10. The journal editor accepts the manuscript and sends it to the publisher for copywriting, typesetting and layout.
11. The manuscript appears on-line as the submitted pdf file.
12. The journal sends the printer's proofs. Correct and return them as quickly as possible.
13. The manuscript appears on-line and, unless it is solely an on-line journal, shortly after in print.

Box 4.2 What is an impact factor and how is it calculated?

Impact factors were *devised* by Eugene Garfield, a great thinker on how to *quantify* the impact of scientific publications (reviewed by Garfield, 2005). Garfield's work with his "Institute of Scientific Information" formed the basis of the company Thomson Scientific, which now manages the definition and calculation of impact factors. Thomson's website has an essay from Eugene Garfield (Garfield, 1994) with the following definition of an impact factor. "An impact factor is a measure of the frequency with which the "average article" in a journal has been *cited* in a particular year or period." This definition may sound straightforward. However, it is not easy to define an "average article". *Furthermore*, the varied frequencies and patterns of publication in different scientific fields greatly complicate the calculation of the impact factors. Indeed, the calculation of impact factors has become so complex that Thomson Scientific could not satisfactorily explain to the executive director of the Rockefeller Press and the executive editors of the Journals of Experimental Medicine and Cell Biology how the impact factors of these journals were determined (Rossner *et al.,* 2007; Rossner *et al.,* 2008).

The calculation of impact factors is obviously a tricky business. Finding the impact factors of a particular journal is also not straightforward. If your organisation has a subscription to Thomson's products, you will be able to access them on-line (isiwebofknowledge.com). If you do not have access, two other approaches may help to find the impact factors of journals you are considering. One is to look on the homepage of the specific journals themselves. *Occasionally*, the journals do state their own impact factor, especially if it is perceived to be high in its particular field. The second is to use the Science Gateway website (www.sciencegateway.org). This extremely useful website lists journal impact factors for subjects ranging from chemistry to political science at www.sciencegateway.org/rank/index.html.

4.2 Planning a scientific manuscript

Section 4.1 discussed step 1 of publishing a scientific manuscript, choosing the journal. In the remainder of this chapter, we will concentrate on step 2, writing, reading and improving the manuscript. Having chosen the journal, the next thing to do is to plan the writing of the different sections. These sections are listed in box 4.3 in their most common order in a scientific manuscript. One *frequent* variation in this order is the position of the "materials and methods" section, as it is occasionally found after the discussion section and not immediately after the "introduction" section. In spite of such differences, the position of the figures and the *tables* remains constant. They are always at the end of the manuscript, separated from the results. The figure legends, which give further details on the figures, are also on a separate page towards the end of the manuscript.

In addition, box 4.3 provides the information which the reader expects in each section of a manuscript. There is nothing special about this information, there are no hidden secrets. Students demonstrate this when they are asked without warning to tell each other about their scientific projects. They always start by describing the subject they are *working* on, why they are doing their work and how they are doing it. They continue with what they have found and finish with what it means. This is the natural way of telling a scientific story, almost *exactly* as in the order shown in box 4.3. Try to keep this in mind when writing your scientific manuscripts.

At the end of their story, the students then summarise their work in one to two sentences. This is the take-home message, the abstract or summary. It is the only difference to the order of a scientific manuscript that is outlined in box 4.3.

Box 4.3   Sections of a scientific manuscript and the information they contain

▌ Title page (Title, affiliations, abbreviations and keywords)
▌ Abstract, summary or synopsis (Take-home message)
▌ Introduction (What is my theme and why am I interested in it?)
▌ Materials and methods, experimental procedures or experimental (How?)
▌ Results (What did I do and what did I find out?)
▌ Discussion (What does it mean?)
▌ Acknowledgements (Who provided advice and materials, who paid for the work?)
▌ References (Whose work is my research based on?)
▌ Tables (The data)
▌ Figure legends (Provide essential details on the data)
▌ Figures (The data)

The natural way of telling a story is well illustrated by the compact article from the journal "Nature" referred to in box 4.4. In the same way as the students, the article begins by answering the questions "what" and "why" (paragraphs one and two). Paragraphs three and four answer the *question* "how". The observations made ("what did I find out") are described in the very brief paragraph five. The story is completed in paragraphs six and and seven in which the meaning of the *observations* is placed into context. This lucid manuscript thus provides all the necessary information without being divided into sections. The author sounds like he is describing his work in the departmental tea-room. This is a sign of a well-crafted manuscript.

An excellent way to begin the planning of your story is to consult the "instructions for authors" or "guidelines for authors" of your chosen journal. Here, you will find the order of the sections as well as the formats for the figures, tables, figure legends and references. The "instructions" or "guidelines" will also detail how many words the abstract may have, the number of keywords requested and whether there is a length limitation for the manuscript as a whole. This may take the form of a certain number of words or figures. The "instructions for authors" can be very dry and difficult to comprehend. If you are unclear on certain aspects, return to browsing in the journal and see how the published articles look. The more you read in your chosen journal, the easier the planning will be. Print a *relevant* article from the selected journal and refer to it whenever you are not sure how the journal deals with a particular point. Note the number of paragraphs in each section and their content. This will give you an estimate of how much you should write in each section.

One useful habit to support the plan is to use the journal's "guidelines for authors" to prepare a style sheet for a new manuscript and to have it with you when writing. On the style sheet, note down items such as whether the journal writes "Figure" or "FIG.", which abbreviations are standard, whether time is written as "min." or "mins" or whether units need a space (10 mg/ml) or not (10mg/ml). Add to the style sheet any abbreviations that you develop yourself. In this way, the manuscript will be *consistent* in itself and with the journal's style. It is much quicker to refer to a style sheet than to scroll through the "guidelines to authors" every time one of these minor, yet vital, points appears.

In which order should you plan the sections of your manuscript? Should they also be written in the order in which they will eventually be submitted in the journal, shown in box 4.3? My *answer* is no. Instead, I recommend that you begin by preparing the figures and tables and by writing the "figure legends" and "results".

Four reasons lie behind this recommendation. First, the figures and *tables* are the most important part of the paper. They are your *data*. They present the advances in knowledge that you wish to communicate to the scientific community.

Second, readers, especially reviewers, know that reading the figures and tables allows them to rapidly assess the quality and novelty of a manuscript. They will begin by looking at the figures and tables on their own. Clearly designed figures and self-explanatory tables will catch the reviewer's interest and encourage them to read the corresponding "results" section. I have yet to meet a reviewer who starts to read a manuscript with the "materials and methods" section.

The third reason for preparing the figures and tables at the start is that you can quickly ascertain whether you have all the data. If you decide that more data are needed, it is better to generate the data before starting to write. There are colleagues and students who seize every opportunity to stop writing and go back to the lab to generate missing data. This strategy is very dangerous. Writing can be painstaking, but running away from it will not make it easier. The manuscript will seem to drag on forever, and there may even be a risk that it will never be finished.

The fourth reason is that the figures automatically give you a plan for writing the "results". Once you have all the figures and tables complete, looking at them in their planned order will give you an idea whether your "results" build a coherent story and how easy it will be to construct your manuscript in a logical way.

The planning and construction of a successful manuscript thus really begin with the generation and *analysis* of the data itself. Try to keep this in mind when designing the experiments. Do I have all the *necessary controls*? Could the experiment be included in a manuscript without further work? Are the data sufficiently reproducible for *inclusion* in a manuscript?

The plan for the order of the remaining sections is shown in box 4.5. The rationale for the position of each section in the list is given in the parts of this chapter that are devoted to each manuscript section. However, if you do not like the order of box 4.5 and want to devise another order or plan, go ahead. The most important thing is that you have a plan and stick to it.

Box 4.4 A manuscript without sections

An excellent example of a manuscript without sections is "Street pigeons in Basel" (Haag-Wackemagel, 1993). The text explains how to interpret the contents of the article.

Box 4.5 Suggested order for planning and writing the sections of a scientific manuscript

- Figures and tables (The data)
- Figure legends (Provide essential details on the data)
- Results (What did I do and what did I find out?)
- Discussion (What does it mean?)
- Introduction (What is my theme and why am I interested in it?)
- Abstract, summary or synopsis (Take-home message)
- Title page (Title, affiliations and keywords)
- Materials and methods, experimental procedures or experimental (How?)
- List and sort the references (Whose work is my research based on?)
- Acknowledgements (Who provided advice and materials, who paid for the work?)
- Title page (Abbreviations)

4.3 Writing a scientific manuscript

Section 4.3 represents the core of this book. It contains a first draft (box 4.6 to box 4.15) of each section of a model scientific manuscript, written according to the plan in box 4.5.

Michael Crichton's book "The Andromeda Strain" provided the inspiration for the experiments and data for the model manuscript. In this famous piece of science fiction, scientists tested thousands of substances before finding an antidote to a killer strain of bacteria from outer space. As I was entering this book into the first draft of the list in section 7.3, the radio happened to carry a story on the need for substances to fight avian influenza virus. Gazing at the South African plants outside my window, I hypothesised that one of these plants contained a substance that could inactivate influenza virus. Using this idea, it was relatively simple to envisage the results of some experiments that could serve as the basis for a model manuscript.

The plan for writing a manuscript in box 4.5 begins with the choice of the data to present and the preparation of the appropriate figures. *Accordingly*, the "data" from the imaginary set of experiments are presented in box 4.6.

Figure 1 is a bar chart showing the effect of three plant extracts on the survival of influenza virus particles. Bar charts are very useful for comparing measurements that just generate one or two data points. In other words, they can be effectively used when too few data points are available to draw a graph. A graph with just two data points is scientifically invalid.

Figure 2, a *graph*, shows that the inactivation seen in figure 1 is *dependent* on the amount of extract added. Note that the axes are clearly labelled and the units stated. A figure without the correct units is not a scientific figure. A further convention for a scientific figure is to plot the *variable* that you systematically modified on the x-axis and the variable that you measured on the y-axis. Keep to this convention; *otherwise*, you may *confuse* the reader. For example, figures 1a and 1b of the paper by Corder *et al.* (2006) do not keep to this convention and are thus very confusing.

Both figures in box 4.6 can be understood without further explanation. In effect, they tell the story contained in the manuscript on their own, with just the information in the clearly labelled axes for support. This is a tremendous aid to the reviewer who consequently does not have to delve into the manuscript to discover the meaning of the figures. Examining carefully whether a figure stands alone is an excellent way of controlling its quality. If a figure is self-explanatory, it is a good one; if not, it must either be improved or omitted.

A further important point to note in both figures is the *presence* of error bars. Error bars allow you and the reader to appreciate the *reliability* of your results and to visualise the *variation* in your experimental system. It is up to you to decide whether the level of variation in your experimental *system* is acceptable. Be aware that the error bars should never extend beyond the difference between the two values you are comparing. If they do, then the degree of error may be too high, the sample size too low or the observed difference insignificant. Whatever the reason, you will have to improve the reproducibility of your system. Whatever *level* of error you finally decide is acceptable, you must of course be able to justify your decision to

the reviewers. We will return to the importance of error bars in the next
section on figure legends.

The preparation of figures nowadays usually involves the use of special-ised computer software, such as Excel, Harvard Graphics Chart, SigmaPlot or SPSS (Statistical Package for the Social Sciences). Make sure that you know how the software *works* and what its limits are. Computers and their software are developed and assembled by humans, so they will have their faults. In 2006, a scientist had to retract five papers (i. e. state that the work was inaccurate) from high quality journals because the software had pro-duced a *model* that was the mirror-image of the correct one (Chang *et al.*, 2006).

If you use Adobe Photoshop or similar software to prepare *images*, photo-graphs or autoradiographs, then read your chosen journal's "instructions for authors" to find out whether there is a passage about which manipu-lations of the images are allowed and which are forbidden. The "Journal of Cell Biology", a journal which obviously has a great interest in avoid-ing wrongful manipulation of images, has very straightforward and lucid guidelines (http://jcb.rupress.org/ifora). The production department of this journal will even specifically look for *evidence* of the manipulation of images. Other journals may ask the reviewers to look out for the telltale signs of the inappropriate modification of images. If you are in doubt, re-strict the processing of an image to that which is absolutely *necessary* and resist all temptation to use the software to make the image "look nice".

Chapter 2 emphasised the importance of omitting needless words. It is equally important to recognise whether a figure is redundant and thus a candidate for *omission*. A figure which does not really show any changes or any differences between two sets of measurements can often be removed and referred to as "data not shown" in the "results" section. *Occasionally*, there is no reference to one of the figures in the "results" section. This is also a sign that the figure is redundant and can be removed. Alternatively, it is sometimes necessary to split a complex figure into two or more parts. *For instance*, a set of measurements over a large range of concentrations or time *periods* may need to be drawn as two separate figures to allow the reader to more rapidly grasp the meaning.

The tables should also be examined to determine whether one or more of them might be deleted or whether some of the content can be condensed. One general rule is that it is not necessary to show the same data both as a figure and a *table*. One of the two is almost always adequate. Another unwritten rule states that data from small tables can often be described in the text. A further guide to drawing clear tables is to look for information that occurs several times in a table. Such information is redundant and can be placed into an extra column or row, so that it occurs just once. Alternatively, this information can be included in the table's title or in a footnote. The manuscript on measuring biodiversity (section 5.3) provides you with a table from which redundant information can be eliminated. Tables 1 and 2 from the article by Wantanabe et al (2004) also provide practice in identifying redundant columns and rows.

Is there a correct number of figures and tables for a manuscript? How can you judge whether you have the correct balance between figures, tables and text? These are tricky questions. The best *answer*, perhaps, is that the manuscript should contain sufficient data to *support* your conclusions. This is one of the most important factors that reviewers assess. If the reviewers feel that not all of the figures are essential to support the conclusions, they will recommend that one or more are removed and thus help the journal to keep to its page limits. One the other hand, if the reviewers feel that there is *insufficient* data, they may ask for more or use this failing as a basis for rejecting the manuscript.

If you really have a substantial amount of data that you feel you must show, you can look into the *possibility* of presenting supplementary material on-line. Most journals now offer this facility of making such material available through their internet portal.

Box 4.6   Figures 1 and 2 for the model manuscript   103

Figure 1

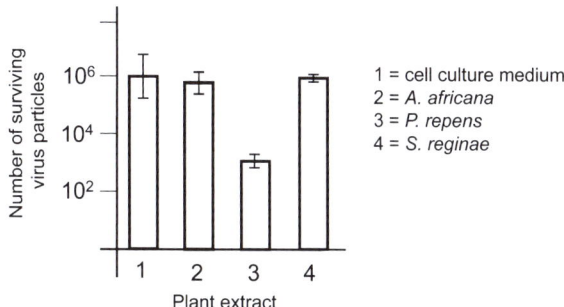

1 = cell culture medium
2 = *A. africana*
3 = *P. repens*
4 = *S. reginae*

Figure 2

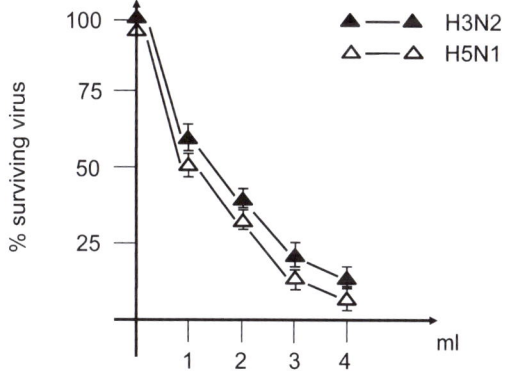

Look *closely* at the figures in the articles in a scientific journal. You will see that each is accompanied by a brief title as well as a short text (termed the "figure legend" or "figure caption"). In general, the title describes either the work performed to generate the data or the outcome of the experiment in the figure. The figure legends then outline in more detail how the experiment was performed and how the data were measured. The information might concern how many times the experiments were performed and report any *deviations* from the standard methods given in the "material and methods" section.

Box 4.7 describes figures 1 and 2 of the *model* manuscript. The title of figure 1 outlines the experiment whereas that of figure 2 states the outcome. The legends provide *relevant* details on how the experiments were performed, including an explanation of how the error bars were determined. It is important for the reader to know whether the error bars represent the range of values measured, the standard deviation, the standard error from the mean or whether they were calculated in some other way. Curiously, scientists often forget to include this important information. *Indeed*, most of the papers in an entire issue of "Nature" were found to lack the information on how the error bars were calculated (Vaux, 2004). To help scientists use and interpret error bars correctly, Dr. Vaux, together with two colleagues, has published a practical introduction to their correct usage (Cumming *et al.*, 2007).

Tables also have a title. However, a convention in scientific writing has developed that tables should be understandable without a legend. Any information which is absolutely necessary to comprehend the table should be added as a footnote. Exercise 5.3 shows you how to use footnotes in tables. Keep footnotes to a minimum, as the tables may otherwise become confusing.

Do not despair if you find it difficult to write concise and accurate figure legends. Almost all scientists, including experienced ones, struggle with this aspect of manuscript writing!

Box 4.7   Figure legends   105

Figure 1. *Incubation* **of three extracts of South African plants with influenza virus particles.** 1 ml of each extract was incubated for 60 min. at room temperature with 10^6 influenza virus particles. The number of surviving virus particles was determined as described in materials and methods. Values represent the average of five separate experiments. Error bars show the standard deviations from the mean.

Figure 2. **Concentration-*dependent* inactivation of two influenza viruses by a *P. repens* extract.** 1 ml of cell culture medium containing 10^6 viral particles of influenza virus H5N1 (open triangles) or H3N2 (closed triangles) was incubated with the volumes of *P. repens* extract *indicated*. The experiment was performed as described in figure 1. Results are expressed as a percentage of the surviving viruses. Values represent the average of three separate experiments. Error bars show the range of values measured.

4.3.3   Write a first draft of the "results"

This section answers the questions "What did I do and what did I find out?" In essence, the text of the "results" section should provide just enough information to understand the interpretation of each *experiment* and the rationale why the next experiment was set up. All further explanation should be reserved for the "discussion" section. In this way, the "results" section will stand on its own, just like the figures. Let us look into the writing of this crucial section in more detail by reflecting a moment on how scientific data is generated. In general, scientists start by formulating a hypothesis or posing a question. They then design an experiment to *test* the *hypothesis* or answer the question. The scientists then take the new measurements or observations and combine or compare them with those in the literature. This may allow an inference that will, in turn, *suggest* the next experiment to test the hypothesis or answer the question. If necessary, *of course*, the hypothesis or question may need to be modified or even completely rephrased after the first experiment. The results of the second experiment are then examined together with information from the literature and new experiments designed. The set of experiments comes to an end when the scientists have enough data on their hypothesis or sufficient answers to their question. The scientists have generated their data in a cycle in which each experiment has built on the previous one. The text of the "results" section should reflect this cycle.

We can see this cycle in the text of the "results" section of the model manuscript (box 4.8). The first paragraph starts with the aim of the experiment and then states why the first experiment was done and what the result was. The text informs the reader which parts of figure 1 to look at and what he or she should see in these parts. In the next two paragraphs, the author describes subsequent experiments, which are based on the results obtained in the first paragraph. The experiment in the second paragraph *strengthens* the *observations* described in the previous one. In contrast, the experiment in paragraph three extends the observations from paragraph one and shows that the *active* extract may be of general use.

Paragraph four sums up the observations and tells the reader that the set of experiments has been brought to an end. It also contains a statement about the interpretation of the results. In the example, the text *anticipates* a possible question about the extraction *process*. Such questions arise when you read through the manuscript and imagine how another scientist might comment on your work. *Effectively*, you are starting to do the task of the reviewer. This approach will immensely strengthen your manuscript.

The "results" section always needs to be co-ordinated with the *figures* and figure legends. To achieve this, print the figures, the figure legends and the text for the "results" and lay them out as shown in box 4.9. This arrangement gives an overview of the critical parts of the manuscript and enables the text to be tailored to the figures and their legends. During this process, it may become necessary to *modify* the figures to make them more appropriate. Just like the text, figures may also need some cycles of refinement before they optimally present the data.

The general tense for the "results" section is the past simple. Most of the verbs in this section of the model manuscript (box 4.8) are in this tense (e.g. "were", "incubated", "inactivated", "failed", "was", "wanted", "tested"). Only five of the 18 sentences in box 4.8 contain verbs that are not in the past simple tense. These verbs are all in the present tense. The first ("supply") represents knowledge that the reader can be expected to know and that will not change. The second ("shows"), in the third sentence of the second paragraph, refers to a figure in the manuscript and is thus clearly an action of the present. Look now at the other ("was") verb in this sentence. It is in the past tense as it is part of the results obtained. The third verb in the present tense, "possesses" in the third paragraph, is in the present tense because it refers directly to a conclusion of the manuscript, namely the ability of the extract to inhibit different influenza virus strains. The final paragraph has two verbs in the present tense, "show" and "conclude". These verbs summarise the actions and thoughts of the author and are again not related to the results obtained in this work. Such exceptions to the past tense are common in the "results" section. Look out for examples when you are reading and use them in your own writing.

Section 2.1.6 suggested that you try to write in the active voice as it is stronger and clearer. Of the 18 sentences in the results section, three are in the passive voice. There would be nothing wrong with writing more sentences in the passive voice. The manuscript would not be rejected for this reason. However, the text would be less vigorous and less *accessible*.

The first draft of the "results" is also the place to lay the groundwork for listing and sorting the references. If you know the exact reference required when writing the first draft, include it. If you do not or are not sure, add the comment "(ref)" at places at which a reference will be required. You can see this comment in the drafts of "results" and subsequent sections. The exact references can be identified and included once all drafts are complete, so that the reference list can rapidly be assembled.

Box 4.8   Results

Plants supply many useful drugs (ref). To *investigate* whether extracts of certain South African plants were able to inactivate influenza virus particles, we incubated influenza virus H5N1, an avian-specific strain, with the extracts shown in figure 1. The *P. repens* extract inactivated about 50% of the influenza virus particles. *In contrast*, the extracts of *A. africana* and *S. reginae* failed to inactivate the virus (Fig. 1). There was also no inactivation with cell culture medium alone.

We wanted to ensure that the *P. repens* extract inactivated the influenza virus particles in a concentration-*dependent* manner. *Accordingly*, we *tested* various volumes of this extract and examined the number of surviving influenza H5N1 virus particles. Figure 2 (open triangles) shows that the inhibition was indeed *dependent* on the volume of the extract. No inactivation with increasing volumes of cell culture medium was observed (data not shown).

To determine whether the *P. repens* extract was also able to inactivate another influenza virus strain, we incubated the extract with influenza virus H3N2, a human-specific strain. The influenza virus H3N2 (Fig. 2, closed triangles) was clearly inactivated in a similar way to the H5N1 influenza virus. Again, no in-activation in the control experiments was observed. *Thus,* the *P. repens* extract possesses a general ability to inactivate influenza virus particles. In addition, six further *P. repens* extracts prepared over a six-month *period* also demonstrated this ability.

In summary, we show here that a plant extract from *P. repens* inactivated virus particles of two strains of influenza virus in a concentration-*dependent* man-ner. In contrast, extracts from *A. africana* and *S. reginae* did not inactivate the influenza virus particles. All three extracts were prepared *similarly. Therefore,* we *conclude* that the inactivation is due to a specific substance found in *P. repens* and not an artefact of the extraction process.

Box 4.9 Arranging the figures, figure legends and results for cohesive writing

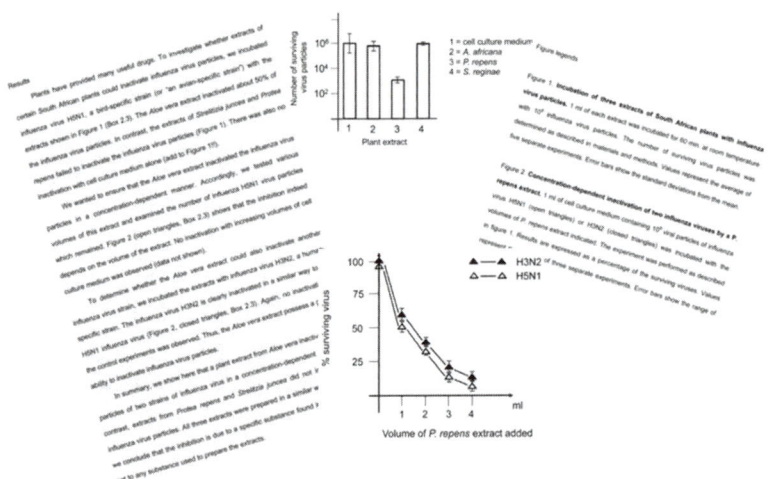

4.3.4 Write a first draft of the "discussion"

In the "results" section, you described what you observed or measured. The logical step now is to discuss what your observations or measure-ments mean. With the "discussion", you are free to answer some or all of the following questions. How do your new findings relate to the present state of knowledge in the literature? How has your work contributed to an advance in knowledge or understanding? Do you wish to give further details on the interpretation of a *particular* experiment? Why was a *particular* experiment done in preference to another? Did you answer the questions you posed at the outset? What have other authors previously published which impacts on the questions you posed? What is the *evidence* in favour of your *hypothesis* and what speaks against it?

Box 4.10 shows the "discussion" of the model manuscript. Clearly, a *genuine* discussion would have more points to discuss and questions to answer. Nevertheless, box 4.10 is a useful demonstration that a compact "discussion" section can be written in just three paragraphs. In the first paragraph, the idea behind the work is reiterated and the main outcome of the work stated. The second paragraph discusses why this particular plant should produce such a substance. In the final paragraph, work for the future is *proposed*, and the potential importance of the discovery for the field is also addressed. Note that direct questions are *asked* to introduce the themes of the second and third paragraphs. This is an effective way of bringing a theme to the reader's attention.

The tenses used in the discussion are the past, present and future. Use past tenses (past simple or perfect) when referring to work in the literature ("have been known" and "was" in the first two sentences in box 4.10) or when you are discussing what you found in your manuscript ("inactivated" in the third sentence in box 4.10). Use the present tense for the "discussion" of the explanations of your observations ("show" in the third sentence) or the implications of your work ("does", "is", "are examining" in the middle paragraph in box 4.10). Any work which you propose to do in addition to the work described should obviously be in the future ("will be directed" in the final paragraph).

The greater freedom available in writing the "discussion" compared to the other sections means that there are more opportunities for falling into a trap. A common one is to start the "discussion" by referring to other people's work. Do not do this. You will make it hard for the reviewer to define the advance in knowledge or to understand what you are reporting. Another trap is to believe that the "discussion" is a review. This is definitely not the case. Some journals even limit the length of the discussion to prevent authors from speculating excessively and becoming too long-winded. Another pitfall is to describe a long list of experiments that should be done to support your results or that might be done in the future. Comments of this kind put ideas into the reviewers' heads. If you are unlucky, they may even ask you to do these experiments.

Box 4.10   Discussion

Substances extracted from plants have long been known to be active against microorganisms (ref). However, the ability of extracts of most South African plants to inactivate influenza virus particles was not known. We show here that a *P. repens* extract inactivated in a concentration-dependent manner two strains of influenza virus that cause disease in humans and birds. Thus, yet another plant can be added to the list of those containing a substance active against micro-organisms.

Why does *P. repens* contain such a substance *capable* of inactivating influenza viral particles? One *possibility* is that the substance is a *product* of a detoxification *pathway* and by chance has anti-viral activity. On the other hand, it may be produced by the plant to protect itself against viruses. To investigate this further, we are currently examining whether related *Protea* species also have anti-viral activity. Related species that produce more of the substance may also be useful in *attempting* to improve the presently unsatisfactory yield.

What is the nature of the *active* substance in *P. repens*? Preliminary experiments (data not shown) *indicate* that the active substance is a novel molecule that can be further explored. Future work will be directed to assessing the clinical potential of this novel substance.

4.3.5   What about writing a combined section entitled "results and discussion"?

Young scientists often pose this question. They point out that a single "results and discussion" section is a more accurate and more natural representation of how they generated the data that they wish to publish. Without being aware of it, they are citing the ideas of Sir Peter Medawar, a Nobel Prize-winning scientist and a staunch supporter of a single section entitled "results and discussion". In chapter 8 of his book "Advice to a Young Scientist", he comments that no-one collects data without stopping to think what it means (Medawar, 1979). He continues that "The separation of 'results' from 'discussion' is a quite arbitrary subdivision of what is in effect a single *process* of thought." In another book, Medawar (1990)

goes on to say that scientists often do experiments in a different order to
that presented in a scientific manuscript. Based on this, he *proposes* that
the separation of "results" and "discussion" *actually* amounts to scientific
fraud.

In spite of Sir Peter's comments and the logic of a single section, a combined section is still the exception rather than the rule. Indeed, many journals insist on this separation, and most scientists seem to prefer separate sections. Why is this so? One reason lies in the extra freedom of the "discussion" section, mentioned in section 4.3.4. A separate discussion section allows greater flexibility to compare new findings with those of others. In a single section, such comparisons can be more problematic. Another reason is that reviewers and readers often want to read just the "results" with the minimum of discussion. This will allow them to *judge* the advance in knowledge and the quality of the research. As experts in the field, they will be able to draw their own conclusions on what the research means.

Despite the above, some journals do permit authors to combine the "results" and "discussion" sections. You may therefore in the future be able to try the combined section approach. To enable you to see the differences between the separated and combined sections, box 4.11 contains a combined "results and discussion" section for the model manuscript. Compare it to the separate sections in boxes 4.8 and 4.10. Which is easier to understand? Which approximates more closely to the way the experiments were done and planned? *Observe* that the single section immediately presents all of the interpretations of a particular experiment, as well as all of the *background* and reasons for setting up the subsequent one. No decisions have to be taken on what has to be kept back for the "discussion section".

One similarity between the separate and combined approaches is the use of direct questions to introduce themes and ideas. In the combined section, posing such questions gives the reader the impression that he or she is listening to how a scientist performed and interpreted the experiment. As a *consequence*, the writing becomes more lively and more interesting. This reflects the more natural representation of experimental work created by the combined "results and discussion" section.

Plants supply many useful drugs (ref). To investigate whether extracts of certain South African plants were able to inactivate influenza virus particles, we incubated influenza virus H5N1, an avian-specific strain, with the extracts shown in figure 1. The *P. repens* extract inactivated about 50% of the influenza virus particles. In contrast, the extracts of *A. africana* and *S. reginae* failed to inactivate the influenza virus particles (Fig. 1). There was also no inactivation with cell culture medium alone.

This experiment *shows* that yet another plant can be added to the list of those containing a substance active against micro-organisms. All three extracts were prepared similarly; therefore, we conclude that the inactivation is due to a specific substance found in *P. repens* and not an artefact of the extraction process.

If the *P. repens* extract *indeed* contains an extract active against influenza virus, it should inactivate the influenza virus particles in a concentration-dependent manner. Accordingly, we tested various volumes of this extract and examined the number of influenza H5N1 virus particles that remained. Figure 2 (open triangles) shows that the inhibition was indeed dependent on the volume of the extract. No inactivation with increasing volumes of cell culture medium was observed (data not shown).

Thus, the extract of *P. repens* contains a substance that can inactivate influenza virus particles in a concentration-dependent manner. Why should *P. repens* contain such a substance? One possibility is that the substance is a product of a detoxification pathway and by chance has anti-viral activity. On the other hand, it may be produced by the plant to protect itself against viruses. To investigate this further, we are currently examining whether related *Protea* species also have anti-viral activity. Related species that produce more of the substance would be useful in attempting to improve the presently unsatisfactory yield.

Can the *P. repens* extract also inactivate a human influenza virus? Such a *property* would significantly increase the importance of the substance in the *P. repens* extract. *To this end*, we incubated the *P. repens* extract with influenza virus H3N2, a human-specific strain. The influenza virus H3N2 (Fig. 2, closed triangles) was clearly inactivated in a similar way to the H5N1 influenza virus. Again, no inactivation in the control experiments was observed (data not shown). Thus, the *P. repens* extract possesses a general ability to inactivate influenza virus particles. In addition, six further *P. repens* extracts prepared over a six-month period also possessed this ability.

These *experiments* demonstrate clearly that a plant extract from *P. repens* can inactivate virus particles of human and avian influenza viruses in a concentration-dependent manner. What is the nature of the active substance? Preliminary experiments (data not shown) indicate that the active substance is a novel molecule that can be further explored. Future work will be directed to assessing the clinical potential of this novel *ingredient*.

4.3.6 Write a first draft of the "introduction"

Write the "introduction" after the "results" and "discussion". These sections will have focussed your thoughts on the *precise* area of your field. You will realise more accurately which parts of the field to introduce and will probably have had several ideas to express concisely your research hypothesis or research question.

The "introduction", like the "discussion", can be written in just three paragraphs. The first outlines the overall scientific area. The second introduces the specific part of the field investigated in the manuscript. The third poses the hypothesis or the research question and briefly outlines the results and conclusions. The "introduction" to the manuscript on plant extracts is constructed in this way (box 4.12). The overall theme in the first paragraph is infectious diseases. The second paragraph concerns the use of natural products to combat such diseases. The third paragraph states the research question and mentions the results.

The tenses used to write the introduction are the present and the past. Thus, the verb in the first sentence of the "introduction" is in the present ("cause") because the sentence is making a general statement. In contrast, in the subsequent sentence, the verb is in the past simple ("were") because the action began and was completed in the past. The situation in the second paragraph is similar, except that the present perfect tense is used in the second sentence ("have been used"). The use of this particular tense signifies that the action is not yet complete. The past tense is also used in the "introduction" to describe what you did in your work. *Thus*, all of the verbs in the sentences of the final paragraph of the "introduction" are in the past.

One small but important point is also illustrated in box 4.12. You may have wondered why in the second paragraph the plant is simply referred to as "xxx" in the introduction. The answer is straightforward. When writing the first draft of any section, try not to stop for details which may take some time to *resolve*. You will have to read and possibly revise the text anyway; searching for details can be done at this time, when you are sure that they will really be used. It is disheartening to spend an hour checking a fact, only to eliminate it in a subsequent version.

Box 4.12   Introduction

Infectious agents cause many human diseases. For instance, human immuno-deficiency virus (HIV) and other communicable diseases were *responsible* for 50% of all deaths in South Africa in the year 2000 (ref).

Substances isolated from plants and fungi are the basis for the treatment of many human diseases (ref). For instance, artemisin from the plant xxx has been used to treat malaria strains *resistant* to previously used drugs (ref).

To *increase* the probability of finding plant extracts active against microorganisms, we decided to examine the huge *variety* of previously untested plants available in southern Africa. We began by investigating the ability of extracts of three South African plants (*Aloe africana*, *Protea repens* and *Strelitzia reginae)* to inactivate influenza virus particles and discovered that the *P. repens* extract was able to do so.

4.3.7   Write a first draft of the "title", the "abstract" and the "keywords"

The "title" and "abstract" are the first parts of your manuscript that the editor, reviewer and reader will see. They are thus crucial to the success of your manuscript. It is vital that they are clear, concise and co-ordinated with each other. The editor of the journal will use the "title" and "abstract" to decide whether the manuscript should be sent out for review and, if so, which reviewers to select. The reviewers will read the "title" and "abstract" to decide whether they feel competent enough to review the manuscript and whether they feel that the manuscript is sufficiently *interesting* to spend their time on a review. The "title" and "abstract" can therefore be considered the visiting card of your manuscript.

The "abstract", the take-home message, is perhaps the most difficult part of the manuscript to write. Journals have limits on the abstract ranging from 100 to 300 words. Accurately summarising a manuscript with several figures and a couple of tables within these limits is a difficult task, even for those who have published extensively.

Here are two suggestions to make abstract writing less difficult. The first is to write your "abstract" at this stage of preparing the manuscript and not leave it to the last minute. Writing the "abstract" early enough will ensure that it undergoes several rounds of editing. The "abstract" will then be in the same style as the main text and accurately reflect the contents.

The second suggestion is to practise writing and correcting them; exercises in chapters 3 and 5 are designed to give you experience in writing and shortening "abstracts".

Two drafts of the "abstract" of the model manuscript are in box 4.13. The first draft has 78 words. 50 words would seem to be a suitable number for this small manuscript. *Accordingly*, the editing suggestions and guidelines in section 2.1.8 and box 3.2 were applied to generate a second draft with 56 words. When shortening the abstract, every word can be considered as a candidate for elimination and each sentence as a candidate for rephrasing. Certain students have told me that they shorten the abstract by specifically removing "the" and "a". This is definitely not an option; the quality of the "abstract" will suffer greatly. Look closely at the improved "abstract" in box 4.13. Can you remove any more words? Would you rephrase any of the sentences? Do you think the abstract is a *succinct* and accurate reflection of the manuscript? The improved version 1.1 (section 4.5.1) of the manuscript later in the chapter shows how to improve the version of the abstract in box 4.13 even further.

The primary tense for the abstract is the past simple to describe what you did and why you did it. The present tense is, however, often used in the final sentence to state the conclusion of the work, point out its importance or stress the take-home message. Both drafts of the abstract in box 4.13 *illustrate* this use of the tenses.

The "title" should be straightforward, comprehensible and, if possible, not contain abbreviations. It should clearly state the contents of your manuscript, but not overstate them. Look at the "titles" of the articles found in your selected journal. Do you find them *interesting*? Are they comprehensible? Do you notice a certain style? Answering all these questions should give you ideas for writing your "title". If you cannot immediately write an satisfactory "title", include your best *attempt* and continue writing. The "title" can undergo refinement just like all other sections of the manuscript. Box 4.14 shows the repeated refinement of the "title" of the model manuscript to obtain one that just about fulfils the above criteria. One fact missing from the "title" is the South African origin of the plants. However, this *vital* information is present in the second version of the "abstract". This detail illustrates the co-ordination of the "title" and the "abstract".

The "title" is placed on the first page (often referred to as the "title page") of the manuscript, along with the names of the authors and their places of work (nowadays termed affiliations). Contact details for the author who submits the manuscript, commonly termed the "corresponding author", are also usually required on this page. The "instructions for authors" of the journals will tell you whether any further information is required. This may include a number of keywords, stating the topics covered in the manuscript, any abbreviations used in the manuscript and sometimes even the abstract.

The keywords for the model manuscript are listed in box 4.14. None of the keywords are present in the "title". Why is this so? Scientists looking for articles relevant to their work use a variety of search terms. The more search terms with which an article can be found, the more *likely* it is to be read by others. If the keywords are the same as those in title, the range of a paper will be *limited. In contrast*, if the keywords are an extension of those in the title, this will amplify the paper's range. *For example*, the keywords in box 4.14 will ensure that the model manuscript is not only found by scientists specifically interested in *P. repens* and influenza virus, but also by scientists working in the broad research areas of respiratory illnesses and natural products.

Box 4.13   Two versions of the abstract

We have investigated the ability of extracts from *Aloe africana*, *Strelitzia reginae* and *Protea repens* to inactivate a human and an avian strain of influenza virus. Only the *Protea repens* extract showed any activity; the addition of increasing amounts of the extract inactivated both the human H3N1 and the avian H5N1 influenza virus strains in a concentration-dependent manner. The extract of *Protea repens* may prove useful in developing a new treatment for the disease caused by these viruses.
Word count: 78

We have investigated the ability of extracts from three South African plants, *Aloe africana*, *Protea repens* and *Strelitzia reginae*, to inactivate influenza virus. Only the *P. repens* extract was able to inactivate influenza viruses from both humans and birds in a concentration-dependent manner. *P. repens* extracts may *prove* useful for developing new treatments for influenza patients.
Word count: 56

Box 4.14 Title and keywords

The development of the title:
▌ Ability of extracts of South African plants to inactivate influenza virus
▌ Extracts of *Protea repens* can inactivate influenza virus particles
▌ Inactivation of influenza virus by a *Protea repens* extract

Keywords: infectious diseases; respiratory illnesses; natural products; anti-viral compounds.

4.3.8 Write a first draft of "materials and methods"

If you have been following the plan in box 4.5, you will be able to see that the first draft of the manuscript is nearly complete. This should motivate you to complete the section on how you did your experiments very swiftly.

Have a look at the "materials and methods" section in box 4.15. The sentences, which are generally in the past simple tense, must be complete and linked to each other logically. Importantly, this section should not read like a cooking recipe (e. g. "Take three plants, freeze in liquid nitrogen and crush"). Scientists assembling their first manuscript occasionally use this style in a mistaken *attempt* to save space. A better way of saving space is to refer to *previous* publications of your group for the standard methods you employed. If you have modified a published protocol, you just need to detail the specific modifications of the published methods and give the reference.

The "materials and methods" section should contain the required details to enable scientists in the field to obtain the reagents and to *repeat* the experiments. Remember that science thrives on the ability to repeat someone's experiments and *verify* the *findings*. Try, therefore, to put yourself in the position of the reader. Have you provided all the information he or she *requires* to successfully *follow* your protocols? Are all concentrations and units given? If the units or formulae require Greek letters or special symbols such as μg for microgram, are they correct? Are all the techniques employed in the "results" section detailed in the "materials and methods" section? Are all the techniques reported in "materials and methods" *actually* used to perform the experiments described in "results"?

There is often interplay between the "material and methods" and the figure legends. The "material and methods" will often state the basics of a technique. The figure legends can then specify the exact *conditions* used in the experiment. Be sure to check the details in these two sections against each other.

Box 4.15   Materials and Methods

H5N1 and H3N2 strains of influenza virus were obtained from the ATCC (American Type Culture Collection, USA) and grown in canine kidney cells as described (refs).

All plants used were obtained from A. Gardener's Plant Supplies (Vienna, Austria). Plant extracts were prepared by crushing 10 g of leaves in liquid nitrogen, allowing the temperature to rise and filtering the resulting liquid through cheesecloth. The filtrates were made up to 10 ml with water, adjusted to neutral pH using the cell culture medium and stored at -70°C.

The anti-viral properties of the extracts were examined by mixing the volumes of the extracts indicated in the *figure* legends with 1 ml of cell culture medium containing 10^6 influenza virus particles. Virus particles were also mixed with the same volumes of cell culture medium. All samples were incubated for 60 min. at room temperature. *Subsequently*, the number of surviving influenza virus particles was determined by placing the treated virus samples on canine kidney cells. The number of cells destroyed, as *detected* by cell staining (ref), is directly *proportional* to the number of surviving viral particles.

If I have seen further,
it is by standing on the shoulders of giants.
ISAAC NEWTON

The references tell the reader which scientific publications you studied to conceive your hypotheses, set up your experiments and support your conclusions. The references reflect your scholarship and your understanding in the field. *Treat* the references with due reverence. Without the work they report, how could you have performed yours?

Students often ask how to recognise when they should *cite* a reference. One answer is that any sentence that specifically refers to the work of others requires a *citation*. Always include the original publications which describe the methods or results to which you are referring. If two groups of workers published on the same topic at about the same time, then cite both sets of authors. *Quote* the publications of your competitors as much as those of your own group. If you quote several references to *support* your idea, do not ignore those that are in opposition. Cite and discuss them in the context of your work. Science and scientific writing require honesty.

In contrast, if a sentence contains general knowledge or information that all scientists in a field will know (e. g. the first sentence in the "introduction" in box 4.12), then a reference is not needed. If you are not sure whether to add a reference or not, add one. The reviewers will not reject a manuscript because the bibliography is too extensive but they may complain if it is too spartan.

Review articles (often referred to as the secondary literature) offer an overview of the field. Include them in the introduction to enable the reader to *delve* deeper into the *background*. Do not use review articles to refer to specific methods or particular results. A reference list containing too many review articles implies that you only have a superficial knowledge of the literature and have not really read the key primary publications of the field.

The section on writing the "results" (section 4.3.3) recommended that you note down where you need references in each section. If you have been doing that, you can now identify the references you wish to cite. Make sure you check all sections of the manuscript, including the figure legends and tables, to see whether you have found all the references you require.

You have a choice for listing and sorting the references so that they conform to the format of the journal. You can type them in and sort them by hand or you can use a program specially developed to manage references. Typing the references in and sorting them by hand is not recommended. This approach is time-consuming, error-prone, inflexible and nerve-wracking. If your supervisor, a co-author, a reviewer or even you yourself decide to insert, modify or delete a reference, you may have to change the order and the numbering of every single one.

In contrast, programs such as Endnote have several advantages. They allow you to introduce the references into the text and format them according to the style of your chosen journal. They provide the accepted abbreviation of each journal in the reference list. A further advantage of such programs is that you can add or delete references from the text once they have been formatted. You can even reformat the references completely without having to redo them all.

The only real hardship that comes with these programs is entering the references to create your own database of references. Typing them in one after another is painful. However, many literature databases such as PubMed, PubMed Central (both from the National Library of Medicine in the USA), Google Scholar, the ISI web of knowledge (Thomson Scientific) or Scopus (Elsevier) allow you to import the references directly into the reference programs. This makes the generation of a reference database, which you can use for the rest of your scientific career, relatively painless.

However you decide to prepare the reference section, remember to check the references carefully. Are the references you have *cited* the correct ones? You may have ten references in your database that all have the same first author. Picking the wrong one is easily done. The reference program should have put the references into the correct format, but was it completely accurate? Check the format you have generated with the one given for the references in the "instructions for authors". Does your chosen journal need the journals' names written in full? If not, are all the abbreviations of the journals' names correct? Are all the page numbers complete? Are the books or book chapters cited in the correct style for the journal? How should the authors be arranged in the list of references? Almost every journal has a certain peculiarity in the reference part.

This very short section can *actually* be written at any time, but writing it towards the end of the final *version* when you know who you wish to thank is a safer policy. You are free to thank anyone who provided advice, helped you with techniques, supplied materials or commented on the manuscript. Despite this freedom, keep the "acknowledgements" simple. "We thank X for critical reading" is perfectly adequate. Always mention the funding agencies that supplied you with the money to carry out your research. Funding agencies often even *stipulate* such an "acknowledgement" in their guidelines. The Austrian Science Fund, for instance, does. *Furthermore*, it only refunds page charges when its support is acknowledged. Page charges are levied by certain journals on authors to cover the printing costs. It is therefore a prudent idea to carefully check at an early stage that the funding body or bodies are mentioned and that the grant numbers are correct. You (or your supervisor) will not panic when you receive the bill for the page charges after the manuscript has appeared on-line or in print. You will be certain that the funding agency will pay and you can pass on the bill.

4.3.11   Write the "abbreviations"

The list of abbreviations is often found on the title page, although some journals may require authors to put them on a separate page. Like the "acknowledgements", you can make this list at any time. For greater accuracy, it is more sensible to prepare it after writing the "materials and methods" as this section usually contains the majority of abbreviations. The list of abbreviations should, of course, be complete and conform to the style of the journal. Bear in mind that most journals accept certain common abbreviations as standard and do not *require* them to be listed. As usual, this information is detailed in the "instructions for authors".

The first version is never the last.

All first drafts of the model manuscript are now complete. The texts from boxes 4.6 to 4.15 can be assembled to produce the first complete version (version 1.0, section 4.4.1). Reaching this stage should always be recognised as a considerable *achievement*. However, it is only now that the time-consuming work of improving the manuscript begins. A first complete version is usually still a long way from the standard required for publication in a scientific journal. Amongst other things, the first version must be checked for coherence, consistency, logic, omissions, *redundancy*, *relevance* and speculation. It is, however, not just a matter of eliminating errors and inconsistencies. It is about imagining how the writing could be improved to help the reader grasp the advance in knowledge that the manuscript documents. It is about describing *exactly* what you did. It is about imagining how the reviewers will *find* your writing. It is about imagining how to modify, redraft and revamp the manuscript so that the reviewers will have a better *chance* of comprehending your thoughts.

Version 1.0 of the model manuscript contains 30 comments and commands numbered in blue to illustrate the improvement process. Some of the comments and commands attend to *poorly* written areas identified through *application* of the suggestions and guidelines contained in section 2.1.8 and box 3.2. Others were introduced by assessing the quality of the assembled manuscript with some of the following questions. Do the "figures", "tables", "figure legends" and "results" fit together? Do the separate sections fit together coherently? Are the sections *consistent* with each other? Are important comments or descriptions about any of the "methods" missing? Do the "materials and methods" and the "results" sections contain similar information? Is some of the text therefore redundant? Is all the information relevant to the manuscript? Does the "introduction" perhaps contain too much information? Does the "discussion" contain too much speculation? Are there parts that can be toned down or removed?

A second set of useful questions to assess quality focuses on imagining how the manuscript could look after *change*. What would happen if this sentence is omitted? What would happen if this section contained more detail here? What would happen if I moved this paragraph from the "results" to the "discussion"? Would this make the text clearer to the reader and thus improve the manuscript? Ask this set of questions once whilst reading the manuscript from front to back and once whilst reading it from back to front, as suggested in box 3.2. The *answers* to these questions are very helpful if you wish to explore other ways of presenting ideas. *Consequently*, they can have a very positive *effect* on the clarity of a manuscript.

Providing answers to the questions mentioned in the *previous* two paragraphs means that a manuscript will go through several versions until it is in a form that can be submitted to a journal. Thus, the first version does not have to be perfect. The sentences may be clumsy and contain too many words. Some details, as in the model manuscript, may be missing. Nevertheless, the first version shows what is missing and how the overall plan is developing.

Think positively about the first version. Do not become concerned that it seems to be *repeating* itself or is incomplete. Only when the first version has been assembled can the author picture the overall framework. A carefully crafted manuscript evolves over time whilst it is being reworked. Often, many excellent ideas only enter manuscripts at later stages. Larger chunks of text that have been deleted from a manuscript can also be seen positively. Save such chunks in a separate file for use in a future research publication or project *application*. It is rare that a text is completely useless. In some cases, deleted text can even contain ideas for an entirely novel *approach* or set of experiments.

I would like to mention two points about the technique of improvement. The first is a reiteration of the plea in section 2.1.8 to do your rewriting and redrafting on a printout. Manuscripts often *remain* incoherent when they are edited solely on a computer monitor. Do not be concerned about the time needed for typing in the changes from the corrected printout. This is never the rate-limiting step in the editing process. *In addition*, during typing, adopt the habit of glancing at each completed paragraph for coloured lines from the spelling and grammar checkers. Fix these problems before moving on. This is an effective way of reducing the time needed later for proof-reading.

The second point concerning improvement technique is to be confident in marking errors and making suggestions and comments on the printout of a manuscript. Use large letters in red ink or another bright colour for your improvements, suggestions and comments. Make a mark at the side of the line concerned and draw a red ring around text which you find too complex.

Inactivation of influenza virus by a *Protea repens* extract (1)

Keywords: infectious diseases; respiratory illnesses; natural products; anti-viral compounds

Abstract

We have investigated the ability of extracts from three South African plants, *Aloe africana*, *Protea repens* and *Strelitzia reginae*, to inactivate influenza virus. Only the P. *repens* extract was able to inactivate influenza viruses from both humans and birds (2) in a concentration-dependent manner. P. *repens* extracts may prove useful for developing new treatments for influenza patients (3).
Word count: 56

Introduction

Infectious agents cause many human diseases (4). For instance, human immunodeficiency virus (HIV) and other communicable diseases were responsible for 50 % of all deaths in South Africa in the year 2000 (ref) (5).

Substances isolated from plants and fungi are the basis for the treatment of many human diseases (ref). For instance, artemisin (6) from the plant xxx (7) has been used to treat malaria strains (8) resistant to previously used drugs (ref) (9, 10).

(11) To increase the probability of finding plant extracts active against microorganisms (12), we decided to examine the huge variety of previously untested plants available in southern Africa. We began by investigating the ability of extracts of three South African plants (*Aloe africana*, *Protea repens* and *Strelitzia reginae*) to inactivate influenza virus particles and discovered (13) that the P. *repens* extract was able to do so (14).

Materials and Methods

H5N1 and H3N2 strains of influenza virus were obtained from the ATCC (American Type Culture Collection, USA) and grown in canine kidney cells as described (refs).

All plants used were obtained from A. Gardener's Plant Supplies (Vienna, Austria). Plant extracts were prepared by crushing 10 g of leaves in liquid nitrogen, allowing the temperature to rise and filtering the resulting liquid through cheesecloth. The filtrates were made up to 10 ml with water (15), *adjusted* to neutral pH using the cell culture medium (15) and stored at −70°C.

The anti-viral properties of the extracts were examined by mixing the volumes of the extracts indicated in the figure legends with 1 ml of cell culture medium containing 10^6 influenza virus particles (16). Virus particles were also mixed with the same volumes of cell culture medium (17). All samples were incubated for 60 min. at room temperature. Subsequently, the number of surviving influenza virus particles was determined by placing the treated virus samples on canine kidney cells. The number of cells destroyed, as detected by cell staining (ref), is directly proportional to the number of surviving viral particles.

1 Make the title active.
2 Omit needless words.
3 Link this sentence to the previous one and write it more clearly and strongly.
4 Write this sentence more clearly and strongly.
5 HIV is irrelevant to this manuscript! More background on influenza virus is required.
6 Check the spelling.
7 The name of the plant must be in the next version.
8 Artemisinin is used to treat patients, not malaria strains.
9 The use of artemisinin is poorly explained.
10 Another example of a plant product is required.
11 Include a sentence making the goal of the work clearer.
12 This word is too general. Find a better one.
13 This word is too strong. Find a better one.
14 Split this sentence into two and make the second part stronger.
15 The descriptions are inaccurate.
16 The sentence is difficult to read and does not fit with the figure legends.
17 State why this was done.

Results

Plants supply many useful drugs (ref) (**18**). To investigate whether extracts of certain South African plants were able to inactivate influenza virus particles, we incubated influenza virus H5N1, an avian-specific strain, with the extracts shown in figure 1 (**19**). The *P. repens* extract inactivated about 50% of the influenza virus particles. In contrast, the extracts of *A. africana* and *S. reginae* failed to inactivate the virus (Fig. 1). There was also no inactivation with cell culture medium alone (**19**).

We wanted to ensure that the *P. repens* extract inactivated the influenza virus particles in a concentration-dependent manner. Accordingly, we tested various volumes of this extract and examined the number of surviving influenza H5N1 virus particles. Figure 2 (open triangles) shows that the inhibition was indeed dependent on the volume of the extract. No inactivation with increasing volumes of cell culture medium was *observed* (data not shown) (**19**).

To determine whether the *P. repens* extract was also able to inactivate another influenza virus strain, we incubated the extract with influenza virus H3N2, a human-specific strain. The influenza virus H3N2 (Fig. 2, closed triangles) was clearly inactivated in a similar way to the H5N1 influenza virus. Again, no inactivation in the control experiments was observed (**19**). Thus, the *P. repens* extract possesses a general ability to inactivate influenza virus particles (**20**). In addition, six further *P. repens* extracts prepared over a six-month period also *demonstrated* this ability (**21**).

In summary, we show here that a plant (**2**) extract from *P. repens* inactivated virus particles of two strains of influenza virus in a concentration-dependent manner. In contrast, extracts from *A. africana* and *S. reginae* did not inactivate the influenza virus particles. All three extracts were prepared similarly (**22**). Therefore, we conclude that the inactivation is due to a specific substance found in *P. repens* and not an artefact of the extraction process (**4**).

Discussion

Substances extracted from plants have long been known to be active against microorganisms (ref) (**23**). However, the ability of extracts of most South African plants to inactivate influenza virus particles was not known (**24**). We show here that a *P. repens* extract (**25**) inactivated in a concentration-dependent manner two strains of influenza virus that *cause* disease in humans and birds. Thus, yet another plant can be added to the list of those containing a substance active against micro-organisms (**26**).

Why does *P. repens* contain such a substance *capable* of inactivating influenza viral particles? One possibility is that the substance is a product of a detoxification pathway and by chance has anti-viral activity. On the other hand, it may be produced by the plant to protect itself against viruses. To investigate this further, we are currently examining whether related *Protea* species also have anti-viral activity. Related species that produce more of the substance may also be useful in attempting to improve the presently unsatisfactory yield.

What is the nature of the active substance in *P. repens*? *Preliminary* experiments (data not *shown*) indicate that the active substance is a novel molecule that can be further explored (**2**). Future work will be directed to assessing the clinical potential of this *novel* substance (**2, 27, 28**).

Acknowledgements

I thank my colleagues for critical reading and the imaginary funding agency for financial support (project 01/07).

2 Omit needless words.
4 Write this sentence more clearly and strongly.
18 This information is superfluous here. Delete the sentence.
19 Provide more details for the reader.
20 This sentence is an over-interpretation. It is also redundant in the light of the first sentence in the next paragraph.
21 This sentence should be strengthened and moved to the next paragraph.
22 This word is inaccurate.
23 The sentence is too complex.
24 Improve the last part of the sentence.
25 State the origin of the plant extract.
26 Mention the extracts that did not work.
27 The word "novel" occurs too often.
28 Give more details on the clinical potential of the substance.

Figure 1. **Incubation of three extracts of South African plants with influenza virus particles.** 1 ml of each extract was incubated for 60 min. at room temperature with 10^6 influenza virus particles (**29**). The number of surviving virus particles was determined as described in materials and methods. Values represent the average of five separate experiments. Error bars show the standard deviations from the mean.

Figure 2. **Concentration-dependent inactivation of two influenza viruses by a *P. repens* extract** (**1**). 1 ml of cell culture medium containing 10^6 viral particles of influenza virus H5N1 (open triangles) or H3N2 (closed triangles) was incubated with the volumes of P. *repens* extract indicated. The *experiment* was performed as described in figure 1. Results are expressed as a percentage of the (**30**) surviving viruses. Values represent the average of three separate experiments. Error bars show the range of values measured.

1   Make the title active.
29 Make *consistent* with the methods section and legend to figure 2.
30 Something is missing here.

Section 4.5.1 contains version 1.1 of the model manuscript. As usual, inserted text is in blue; rejected text has been deleted.

Compare the sections of versions 1.0 and 1.1 one by one. This will give you experience in recognising parts of a manuscript needing work and allow you to *envisage* ways to improve them. You can continue this process by examining version 1.1 for areas that need further attention and proposing an appropriate text. After all, it is only version 1.1, so there still is plenty of scope for diligent refinement to increase the accuracy, precision and rigour of the writing..

How close is the quality of version 1.1 to that required for submission to a journal? One to two major polishing steps would probably be necessary to make the sentences fit together better and to remove needless words. In version 1.1, for example, there still seems to be some repetition between the final paragraphs of the results and the first paragraph of the discussion. This problem would definitely need attention before submission. Only when authors have addressed such issues is a manuscript nearing completion. One effective approach to find out how far a manuscript has advanced is to read it out loud to yourself or to use the read aloud tool in Adobe's Acrobat reader. Problematic passages are often easier to find this way. In spite of these tips, it is only when a journal rejects a manuscript because it appears unfinished that you will start to acquire the experience to *judge* for yourself when a manuscript is ready for submission. In the words of Peter Loewen, a Canadian scientist, "At some point, there comes a time when you just have to submit the manuscript and see what the reviewers think!"

This comment stresses another important point in writing scientific English, namely that a manuscript will never be perfect. There will always be something that can be rephrased or improved upon. In a way, writing a scientific manuscript is like evolution. Evolution does not produce something that is perfect, it just produces something that *works*. Your manuscript has to *survive* in the harsh environment of the editorial department of a journal. It does not have to be perfect to do this.

A *Protea repens* extract inactivates influenza virus

Keywords: infectious diseases; respiratory illnesses; viral pathogens; natural products; anti-viral compounds

Abstract

We have investigated the ability of extracts from three South African plants, *Aloe africana*, *Protea repens* and *Strelitzia reginae*, to inactivate influenza virus. Only the *P. repens* extract was able to inactivate human and avian influenza viruses in a concentration-dependent manner. The *P. repens* extract may therefore contain novel substances for treating influenza virus infections.
Word count: 55

Introduction

Infectious agents are a major *cause* of human mortality. The global outbreak of influenza virus in 1918 and 1919 led to at least 20 million deaths (Yewdell and García-Sastre, 2002). At present, outbreaks of human influenza virus are partially controlled by vaccination. However, currently circulating influenza viruses of birds may have the potential to cause serious epidemics in humans in the future (Uyeki, 2008).

Substances isolated from plants and fungi are the basis for the treatment of many human diseases (Rishton, 2008). Digitalis, isolated from the foxglove plant, has been used to treat heart disease for over two centuries (Wade, 1986). More recently, artemesinin, a substance isolated from the plant *Artemisia annua*, has been used to treat patients infected with the malaria parasite, *Plasmodium falciparum* (White, 2008).

We therefore decided to examine whether plant extracts contained substances active against currently circulating human and avian influenza viruses. To increase the probability of *finding* plant extracts active against these pathogens, we decided to examine the huge variety of previously untested plants available in southern Africa. We began by investigating the ability of extracts of three South African plants (*Aloe africana*, *Protea repens* and *Strelitzia reginae*) to inactivate influenza virus. The results revealed that the *P. repens* extract possessed such an activity.

Materials and Methods

H5N1 and H3N2 strains of influenza virus were obtained from the ATCC (American Type Culture Collection, USA) and grown in canine kidney cells as described (Green, 1962; Ho et al., 1976).

All plants used were obtained from A. Gardener's Plant Supplies (Vienna, Austria). Plant extracts were prepared by crushing 10 g of leaves in liquid nitrogen, allowing the temperature to rise and filtering the resulting liquid through cheesecloth. The filtrates were filled up to 10 ml with cell culture medium, adjusted to neutral pH with sodium hydroxide and stored at −70°C.

The anti-viral properties of the extracts were examined as follows. 1 ml of cell culture medium containing 10^6 influenza virus particles was incubated with 1, 2, 3 or 4 ml of the plant extracts as indicated in the legends to figures 1 and 2. As a control, virus particles were also mixed with the same volumes of cell culture medium. All samples were incubated for 60 min. at room temperature. Subsequently, the number of surviving influenza virus particles was determined by placing the treated virus samples on canine kidney cells. The number of cells destroyed, as detected by cell staining (Ho et al., 1976), is directly proportional to the number of surviving viral particles.

Results

To investigate whether extracts of certain South African plants were able to inactivate influenza virus particles, we incubated influenza virus H5N1, an avian-specific strain, with the extracts shown in figure 1, columns 2 to 4. Surviving virus particles were determined as described (Ho *et al.*, 1976). The *P. repens* extract inactivated about 50% of the influenza virus particles. In contrast, the extracts of *A. africana* and *S. reginae* failed to inactivate the virus (Fig. 1). As a control, we incubated the influenza virus particles with cell culture medium without plant extracts. Their number remained unchanged (Fig. 1, column 1).

We wanted to ensure that the *P. repens* extract inactivated the influenza virus particles in a concentration-dependent manner. Accordingly, we tested various volumes of this extract and examined the number of surviving influenza H5N1 virus particles. Figure 2 (open triangles) shows that the inhibition was indeed dependent on the volume of the *P. repens* extract added. In contrast, no inactivation of the H5N1 influenza virus particles was *observed* with increasing volumes of cell culture medium alone (data not shown).

To determine whether the *P. repens* extract was also able to inactivate another influenza virus strain, we incubated the extract with influenza virus H3N2, a human-specific strain. The influenza virus H3N2 (Fig. 2, closed triangles) was clearly inactivated in a similar way to the H5N1 influenza virus. Again, no inactivation in the control *experiments* with cell culture medium alone was observed (data not shown).

In summary, an extract from *P. repens* inactivated virus particles of two strains of influenza virus in a concentration-dependent manner. In addition, six further *P. repens* extracts prepared over a six-month period also reproducibly inactivated influenza virus particles. In contrast, extracts from *A. africana* and *S. reginae* did not inactivate the influenza virus particles. All three extracts were prepared according to the same protocol. Therefore, we conclude that the inactivation resulted from a specific substance or substances present in the *P. repens* extract and not from an artefact of the extraction process.

Discussion

The anti-microbial activity of certain plant and fungal extracts has been known for many years (Wainwright, 1987). However, the ability of extracts of most South African plants to inactivate influenza virus particles had not been *investigated*. We show here that an extract of *P. repens*, an indigenous South African plant, inactivated in a concentration-dependent manner two strains of influenza virus that cause disease in humans and birds. Thus, yet another plant can be added to the list of those containing a substance active against micro-organisms. In contrast, extracts from *A. africana* and *S. reginae* did not inactivate the influenza virus particles.

Why does *P. repens* contain such a substance capable of inactivating influenza viral particles? One possibility is that the substance is a product of a detoxification pathway and by chance has anti-viral activity. On the other hand, it may be produced by the plant to protect itself against viruses. To investigate this further, we are currently examining whether related *Protea* species also have anti-viral activity. Related species that produce more of the substance may also be useful in attempting to improve the presently unsatisfactory yield.

What is the nature of the active substance in *P. repens*? Preliminary experiments (data not shown) indicate that the active substance is a novel molecule. Future work will *assess* the clinical *potential* of this substance against influenza virus infections.

Acknowledgements

I thank my colleagues for critical reading and the imaginary funding agency for financial support (project 01/07).

References

Green, I.J. (1962) Serial Propagation of Influenza B (Lee) Virus in a Transmissible Line of Canine Kidney Cells. Science **138**, 42–43.

Ho, P.P.K., Young, A.L. and Truehaft, M. (1976) Plaque Formation with Influenza Viruses in Dog Kidney Cells. J. Gen. Virol. **33**, 143–145.

Rishton, G. (2008) Natural Products as a *Robust* Source of New Drugs and Drug Leads: Past Successes and Present Day Issues. Am. J. Cardiol. **101**, 43D–49D.

Uyeki, T.M. (2008) Global Epidemiology of Human Infections with Highly Pathogenic Avian Influenza A (H5N1) Viruses. Respirology **13**, Suppl. 1:S2–9.

Wade, O.L. (1986) Digoxin 1785–1985. I. Two Hundred Years of Digitalis. J. Clin. Hosp. Pharm. **11**, 3–9.

Wainwright, M. (1987) History of the Therapeutic Use of Crude Penicillin. Med. Hist. **31**, 41–50.

White, N.J. (2008) Qinghaosu (Artemisinin): the Price of Success. Science **320**, 330–334.

Yewdell, J. and García-Sastre, A. (2002) Influenza Virus Still Surprises. Curr. Opin. Microbiol. **5**, 414–418.

Figure 1. **Incubation of three extracts of South African plants with influenza virus particles.** 1 ml of cell culture medium containing 10^6 influenza virus particles was incubated for 60 min. at room temperature with 1 ml of each extract. The number of surviving virus particles was determined as described in materials and methods. *Values* represent the average of five separate experiments. Error bars show the standard deviations from the mean.

Figure 2. **The *P. repens* extract inactivates influenza virus strains in a concentration-dependent manner.** 1 ml of cell culture medium containing 10^6 viral particles of influenza virus H5N1 (open triangles) or H3N2 (closed triangles) was incubated with the volumes of *P. repens* extract indicated. The experiment was performed as described in *figure* 1. Results are expressed as a percentage of the number of surviving viruses. Values represent the average of three separate experiments. Error bars show the range of values measured.

4.6   Take-home messages from chapter 4

▮ Put your greatest effort into presenting and describing the data.
▮ The figures and tables should be *comprehensible* without reference to the text.
▮ Remember that you are writing for anonymous readers, not for friends or colleagues. You are not writing for your supervisor who understands your theme.
▮ The first draft will be imperfect.
▮ The abstract is the first part of the manuscript to be read. It may be the only part that some readers encounter.
▮ Keep the following words in your head when improving your manuscript: rearrange, rewrite, rephrase, simplify, polish.
▮ Always read your work as a reviewer might.
▮ Read aggressively to change a manuscript, not defensively to avoid change.

Articles

Adams, P., Kandiah, E., Effantin, G., Steven, A. C., and Ehrenfeld, E. (2009). Poliovirus 2C protein forms homo-oligomeric structures required for ATPase activity. J. Biol. Chem **284**, 22012-22021.

Chang, G., Roth, C. B., Reyes, C. L., Pornillos, O., Chen, Y. J. and Chen, A. P. (2006) Retraction. Science **314**, 1875.

Cumming, G., Fidler, F. and Vaux, D. L. (2007) Error Bars in Experimental Biology. J. Cell Biol. **177**, 7–11.

Haag-Wackemagel, D. (1993) Street Pigeons in Basel. Nature **361**, 200.

Rossner, M., Van Epps, H. and Hill, E. (2007) Show Me the Data. J. Cell Biol. **179**, 1091–1092.

Rossner, M., Van Epps, H. and Hill, E. (2008) Irreproducible Results: A Response to Thomson Scientific. J. Cell Biol. **180**, 254–255.

Vaux, D. L. (2004) Error Message. Nature **428**, 799.

Watanabe, S., Watanabe, T., Noda, T., Takada, A., Feldmann, H., Jasenosky, L. and Kawaoka Y. (2004) Production of novel ebola virus-like particles from cDNAs: an alternative to Ebola virus generation by reverse genetics. J Virol. **78**, 999–1005.

Books

Crichton, M. (1970) The Andromeda Strain.

Medawar, P. (1979) Advice to a Young Scientist.

Medawar, P. (ed. Pyke, D.) (1990) The Threat and the Glory: Reflections on Science and Scientists.

Websites

Garfield, E. (1994) The Thomson Reuters Scientific Impact Factor.
www.thomsonreuters.com/products_services/science/free/essays/impact_factor

Garfield, E. (2005) The Agony and the Ecstasy – The History and Meaning of the Journal Impact Factor.
http://garfield.library.upenn.edu/papers/jifchicago2005.pdf

www.endnote.com

www.scopus.com

http://isiwebofknowledge.com

http://jcb.rupress.org/ifora

www.pubmed.gov

www.pubmedcentral.nih.gov

www.sciencegateway.org

www.sciencegateway.org/rank/index.html

http://scholar.google.com

www.sigmaplot.com

www.spss.com

Experience is the name we give to our mistakes.
OSCAR WILDE

Chapter 4 presented ideas for writing, refining and improving a scientific manuscript. Chapter 5 contains six exercises to practise using these ideas. The second and fourth exercises invite you to discuss your point of view on two contemporary themes. The other four exercises provide opportunities to imagine experiments for your own model manuscripts. References mentioned in the exercises are given at the end of the chapter.

Each exercise also has a manuscript of a former student for you to improve and summarise. As in chapter 3, comments and commands numbered in blue initiate the improvement process. An improved version of each manuscript with a summary follows immediately afterwards.

During the preparation of this book, students and colleagues tried the exercises and provided some stimulating feedback. One comment of a Chinese scientist intrigued me greatly. She showed me her suggestions and then exclaimed earnestly, "These exercises are hard!" The stress was on the final word. My response was that the exercises demonstrate the level of writing necessary for scientific publication. Manuscripts of young scientists must achieve this standard. There are no exceptions for novices, there are no journals that accept manuscripts only from young scientists. *Attempting* the exercises in this chapter will help you to more rapidly reach the standard of an experienced scientist.

5.1   Improving the quality of bread

Finding the conditions for boiling the perfect egg is often taken as an *illustration* of the scientific process. The first exercise takes this *idea* one step further. Imagine that you have been trying to *develop* a new ingredient or a new *process* for baking bread. As a consumer, you could introduce a new ingredient to make the bread more nourishing, more long-lasting or more appealing to the eye. If you are interested in ecology or the environment, you might *search* for processes that reduce the baking time and thus lower the burden on the environment. You could even help professors who forget about their baking by developing a substance that lengthens the time taken for the bread to catch fire. If you are British, you might want your new substance or process to generate a bread with the consistency of a damp towel without having to use any organic materials whatsoever.

Write a manuscript about the development of your new process or the properties of your new *ingredient*. Use the model manuscript in chapter 4 as a template to *describe* an experiment that measures the effect of your process or ingredient. Your manuscript will need a title, an abstract as well as the sections "introduction", "materials and methods", "results" and "discussion".

5.1.1 A pyramidal bread box keeps bread fresh longer

Abstract

Pyramids are known to preserve food and living (1) material from deteriorating (1). In this study (2) pyramidal-shaped (3) and hemispherical-shaped bread boxes of different materials were tested for their conservation properties of (1) bread. The pyramids conserved (4) bread from one to eight days longer than the hemispheres. The effect (3) was only missing (5) in steel-made (1) bread boxes, confirming the observation (3) that electrically conducting materials can not develop the pyramid power. Thanks to this study, it is now possible (3) to keep bread fresh for up to fourteen days.

Introduction

The pyramid power

During the last century, the so-called "pyramid power" was discovered and extensively studied. According to the (1) theory, pyramids generate a sort (1) of energy which (1) derives simply from their shape. Especially pyramids that are proportional to the ancient Cheops Pyramid in Egypt show this interesting phenomenon. They (6) generate high magnetic fields, can sharpen up (3) old (1) razor blades, increase intellectual abilities of humans (5) and they are able to (3) conserve colours, perfumes and shapes. E.g., (7) fruits and flowers put (1) inside a pyramid do not deteriorate as they would do at (1) the air or in another container (5), but they slowly shrink, without loosing (8) their colour, odour and (1) taste. The shape of the pyramids is thought to be responsible for their conserving capacities and **(1, 5)** this could explain the extraordinary state of Egyptian mummies found in the Cheops Pyramid.

Bread freshness

A big **(1)** criterion for bread quality is its freshness, which should be conserved **(1)** as long as possible. Under perfect conditions (i. e. inside a common bread box at room temperature and dry storage), white bread keeps **(1)** fresh for two days, while black bread in **(3)** general lasts up to 6 days. The conservation method critically **(4)** determines the freshness of the product.

In this study **(2)** we constructed pyramidal and hemispherical bread boxes of different materials and compared their conservation properties. Our hypothesis was **(1, 3)** that the pyramid-shaped boxes would conserve bread longer than hemisphere-shaped boxes **(1)**, according **(1)** to the power of pyramids. The shape of the hemisphere was chosen as a control to the pyramidal shape and should **(3)** represent a common **(1)** bread box.

Material and Methods

Tested bread types

Three bread types were tested: white bread, rye bread and bread rolls. White bread consisted of 100 % wheat flour. Rye bread had a minimum rye flour content of 70 % and could additionally contain seeds. Bread rolls were small **(9)** round breads or plaited buns containing different amounts of wheat flour and other cereal flours. Seeds were allowed to be **(3)** in the crumb and on the crust, while salted crusts were excluded. All bread types contained yeast; rye bread additionally contained sourdough. The white and rye bread samples weighed 0.5 kg **(10)** and were loaf-shaped. The bread rolls weighed 150 g **(10)**. All bread samples were checked for fourteen **(11)** days every 24 **(10)** hours (counted from the moment **(1)** when the bread came out of the oven).

Bread boxes

Bread boxes of two shapes were constructed and tested: hemispherical boxes (radius 29.32 cm) and pyramidal boxes (quadratic basis 46.1 cm, height 29.32 cm). The dimensions of the pyramid-shaped boxes were proportional to the ones **(3)** of the Cheops Pyramid (quadratic basis 230.33 m, height 146.59 m **(10)**). The height of the hemispherical boxes equalled the height **(3)** of the pyramidal ones. Four materials were used to construct the bread boxes: untreated birch wood, unglazed ceramic, plastic (100 % melamin), and stainless steel. The latter was the only electrically conducting material and served as a control, since **(1)** the pyramid power is said to be confined to electrically insulating material. In sum **(1)**, 8 **(11)** bread boxes were built: 4 **(11)** hemispherical boxes (one per material) and 4 **(11)** pyramidal boxes (one per material).

Arrangement of the bread boxes

All eight bread boxes were placed in a room previously checked for its missing **(5)** electric and magnetic fields that could interfere with the pyramids. The distance between the bread boxes was 1 m **(10)** (calculated from the outer edge of the boxes); boxes were placed in 2 **(11)** rows. In a third row **(2)** bread samples laid **(12)** free in the air. The pyramids as well as **(3)** the bread samples were adjusted **(1)** to the magnetic North-Pole, as the Cheops Pyramid does **(4)**.

Evaluation of the bread freshness

The freshness of the bread was defined as the sum of the following criteria: odour **(1)** (ranging from "intensive"=100% to "weak"=0%), taste ("rich"=100% to "flavourless"=100%), crust ("crispy"=100% to "soft"=0%), crumb ("tender"=100% to "dry"=0%), and aspect ("attractive"=100% to "un-attractive"=0%). 100 women and 100 men (25–45 years old) were asked to taste all types of bread samples for 14 days and fill out a questionnaire for the above-mentioned quality criteria. The **(3)** test persons were not informed how the bread samples had been conserved.

The HMF-index

To compare the freshness of the bread samples **(2)** the half-maximal freshness index (HMF) was defined as the day after baking the bread at which the freshness reached fifty percent **(3)** of its original value.

Results and Discussion (13)

The freshness of all bread types was best conserved in the pyramidal bread boxes (Fig.1 a–c). This was true **(1)** for all tested bread box materials (data not shown) besides **(1)** for the steel pyramids, where **(1)** the conservation in a pyramid equalled **(5)** the conservation in a hemisphere (Fig. 1 d). Ceramic revealed to be **(3)** the best material for bread conserva-

tion as compared to wood, plastic and steel (3), both for hemispherical and
pyramidal boxes (data not shown).

For white bread, the HMF-index laid at (1) day 3 in the hemisphere and at (3) day 5 in the pyramid. The HMF of rye bread was at (3) day 6 in the hemisphere and at day 14 in the pyramid. Small bread rolls reached their HMF before day 2 when conserved in hemispheres, and at day 3 when conserved in a pyramid box (Fig. 1 c).

This study confirms the observation that the simple shape of pyramids is able to keep food fresh longer. For the first time (2) pyramids of different materials were systematically tested for their ability to preserve bread from getting old (3, 14). Our results prove (15) that the power of pyramids only appears in electrically insulating materials like (1) ceramic, wood and plastic, while pyramids made of stainless steel did not work (4) better than steel hemispheres (5).

The production of pyramidal shaped bread boxes made of unglazed ceramic would be an innovating and future oriented idea (1). Hotels and restaurants could profit from longer bread conservation (especially for rye bread). If enough space is given (3), the bread pyramid would also be the best conservation method at home. For this purpose, also smaller pyramids are going to be tested soon (3).

1   A word is missing or the present one needs improving (e. g. big, do, make).
2   Look at the use of commas, situation 3, in section 1.2.2.1
3   Omit needless words.
4   Improve your text with suggestions and questions in Box 3.2.
5   Sentence is too complex. Keep it simple; try just one idea per sentence.
6   What does the pronoun (e. g. it, they, this, that, these) refer to?
7   Avoid using abbreviations as part of the sentence.
8   Use a spellchecker or check your spellchecker.
9   Look at the use of commas in section 1.2.2.1.
10 Keep both the units and the spacing uniform.
11 There is a convention to write out numbers up to twelve.
12 The word you need is the past tense of lie.
13 These sections can be separated.
14 Avoid "get".
15 Nothing can be proven experimentally.
16 Error bars need explanation.

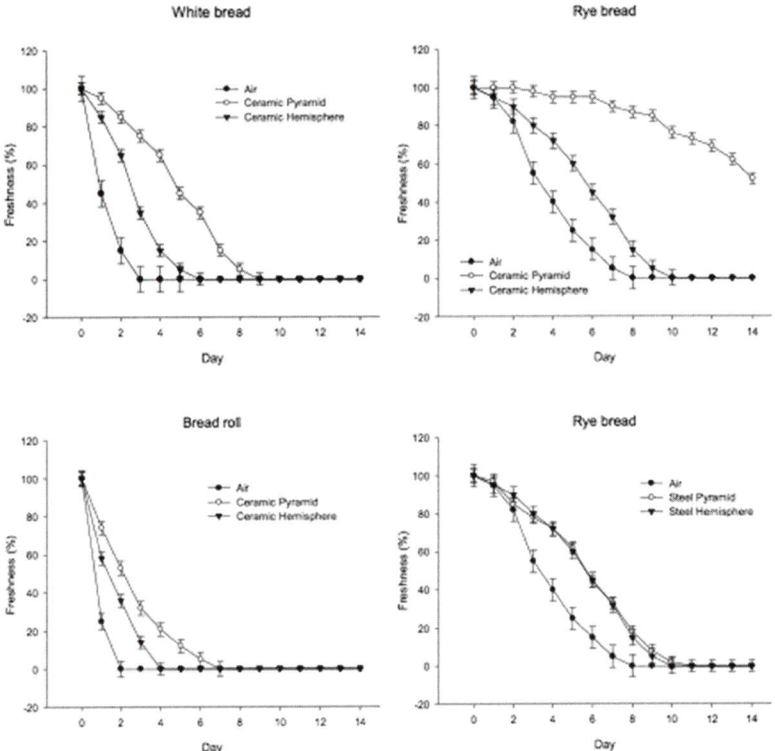

Fig. 1: Freshness change of different bread types (white bread, rye bread, bread roll) by **(1)** conservation in a **(3)** pyramid-shaped or hemisphere-shaped bread box made of unglazed ceramic (a–c) or stainless steel (d). The pyramid was the best shape to keep bread longer fresh in **(3)** all tested bread types and for all tested box materials (data from wood- and plastic-boxes are not shown). Rye bread diminished to **(3)** 50 % of its initial freshness only after 14 days. When the bread box was made of stainless steel, the pyramidal shape did not preserve rye bread from getting **(14)** old and the results equalled the **(3)** conservation in a hemisphere-shaped box **(16)**.

Abstract

Pyramids are known to preserve food and prevent organic material from decomposing. In this study, pyramidal and hemispherical-shaped bread boxes of different materials were tested for their ability to conserve bread. Pyramids were found to conserve bread from one to eight days longer than hemispheres. No conservation was however found in steel-made pyramidal bread boxes, confirming that electrically conducting materials can not develop the pyramid power. This work enables bread to be kept fresh for up to fourteen days.

Introduction

The pyramid power

During the last century, the so-called "pyramid power" was discovered and extensively studied. According to this theory, pyramids generate a type of energy that derives simply from their shape. Especially pyramids that are proportional to the ancient Cheops Pyramid in Egypt show this interesting phenomenon. Such pyramids generate high magnetic fields, can sharpen blunt razor blades and increase intellectual abilities of humans. Further, such pyramids can conserve colours, perfumes and shapes. For example, fruits and flowers placed inside a pyramid do not deteriorate as they would do in the air or in another container; in contrast, they slowly shrink, without losing their colour, aroma or taste. The shape of the pyramids is thought to be responsible for their conservation capacities; accordingly, this could explain the extraordinary state of Egyptian mummies found in the Cheops Pyramid.

Bread freshness

An appreciable criterion for bread quality is its freshness, which should be maintained as long as possible. Under perfect conditions (i. e. inside a common bread box at room temperature and dry storage), white bread remains fresh for two days, while black bread generally lasts up to 6 days. Critically, the conservation method determines the freshness of the product.

In this study, we constructed pyramidal and hemispherical bread boxes of different materials and compared their conservation properties. We postulated that was that the pyramid-shaped boxes would conserve bread longer than hemisphere-shaped ones, given the power of pyramids. The shape of the hemisphere was chosen as a control to represent a standard bread box.

Material and Methods

Tested bread types

Three bread types were tested: white bread, rye bread and bread rolls. White bread consisted of 100 % wheat flour. Rye bread had a minimum rye flour content of 70 % and could additionally contain seeds. Bread rolls were small, round breads or plaited buns containing different amounts of wheat flour and other cereal flours. Seeds were allowed in the crumb and on the crust, while salted crusts were excluded. All bread types contained yeast; rye bread additionally contained sourdough. The white and rye bread samples weighed 500 g and were loaf-shaped. The bread rolls weighed 150 g. All bread samples were checked for 14 days every 24 hours (counted from the time when the bread came out of the oven).

Bread boxes

Bread boxes of two shapes were constructed and tested: hemispherical boxes (radius 29.32 cm) and pyramidal boxes (quadratic basis 46.1 cm, height 29.32 cm). The dimensions of the pyramid-shaped boxes were proportional to those of the Cheops Pyramid (quadratic basis 230.33 m, height 146.59 m). The height of the hemispherical boxes equalled that of the pyramidal ones. Four materials were used to construct the bread boxes: untreated birch wood, unglazed ceramic, plastic (100 % melamin), and stainless steel. The latter was the only electrically conducting material and served as a control, as the pyramid power is said to be confined to electrically insulating material. In summary, eight bread boxes were built: four hemispherical boxes (one per material) and four pyramidal boxes (one per material).

Arrangement of the bread boxes

All eight bread boxes were placed in a room previously shown to lack electric and magnetic fields that could interfere with the pyramids. The distance between the bread boxes was 1 m (calculated from the outer edge of the boxes); boxes were placed in two rows. In a third row, bread samples lay free in the air. Both pyramids and the bread samples were aligned as the Cheops Pyramid to the magnetic North-Pole.

The freshness of the bread was defined as the sum of the following criteria: aroma (ranging from "intensive"=100 % to "weak"=0 %), taste ("rich"=100 % to "flavourless"=100 %), crust ("crispy"=100 % to "soft"=0 %), crumb ("tender"=100 % to "dry"=0 %), and aspect ("attractive"=100 % to "unattractive"=0 %). 100 women and 100 men (25–45 years old) were asked to taste all types of bread samples for 14 days and fill out a questionnaire for the above-mentioned quality criteria. Test persons were not informed how the bread samples had been conserved.

The HMF-index

To compare the freshness of the bread samples, the half-maximal freshness index (HMF) was defined as the day after baking the bread at which the freshness reached half its original value.

Results

The freshness of all bread types was best conserved in the pyramidal bread boxes (Fig.1 a–c). This was observed for all tested bread box materials (data not shown) except for the steel pyramids in which the conservation in a pyramid *was equal* to the conservation in a hemisphere (Fig. 1 d). Ceramic was the best material for bread conservation for both hemispherical and pyramidal boxes (data not shown).

For white bread, the HMF-index was found to be day 3 in the hemisphere and day 5 in the pyramid. The HMF of rye bread was day 6 in the hemisphere and day 14 in the pyramid. Small bread rolls reached their HMF before day 2 when conserved in hemispheres, and at day 3 when conserved in a pyramid box (Fig. 1 c).

Discussion

This study confirms the observation that the simple shape of pyramids is able to keep food fresh longer. For the first time, pyramids of different materials were systematically tested for their ability to preserve bread. Our results demonstrate that the power of pyramids only appears in electrically insulating materials such as ceramic, wood and plastic. In contrast, pyramids made of stainless steel failed to conserve bread better than steel hemispheres.

The production of pyramidal shaped bread boxes made of unglazed ceramic would be an innovative idea with implications for the future **(1)**.

Hotels and restaurants could profit from longer bread conservation (especially for rye bread). With enough space, the bread pyramid would also be the best conservation method at home. For this purpose, smaller pyramids will also be tested.

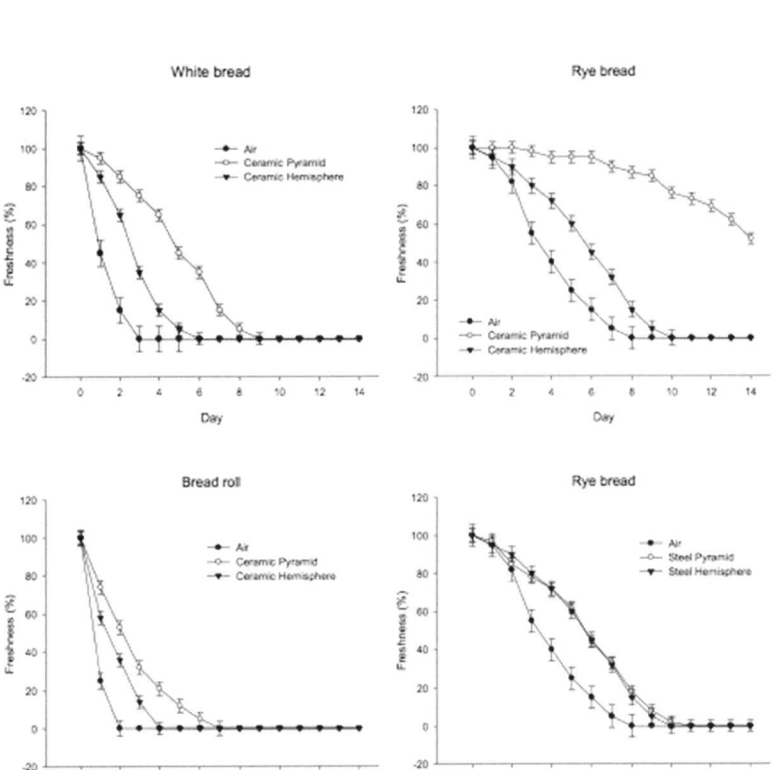

Fig. 1: Freshness change of different bread types (white bread, rye bread, bread roll) on conservation in pyramid shaped or hemisphere shaped bread boxes made of unglazed ceramic (a–c) or stainless steel (d). The pyramid was the best shape to keep bread longer fresh for all tested bread types and for all tested box materials (data from wood- and plastic-boxes are not shown). Rye bread lost 50 % of its initial freshness only after 14 days. When the bread box was made of stainless steel, the pyramidal shape did not preserve rye bread from becoming old and the results equalled those for conservation in a hemisphere-shaped box. Error bars represent standard error of the mean.

All human activity *affects* the environment. We saw in the text in box 4.4 that even the activity of feeding pigeons can be described as being "eco-pathological". Humans have been debating the extent of these effects on the environment for many years. In the late 19th century, the Viennese believed the rise in the number of horse-drawn carriages would *cause* their town to disappear in a mound of horse excrement. Forty to fifty years ago, people feared that human activity was leading to a new ice age. Twenty to thirty years ago, we heard that acid rain from heavy industry was about to *destroy* human life as we know it. Nowadays, pages of newsprint are devoted to the emissions of carbon dioxide. Increasing levels of this gas are expected to retain more heat in the atmosphere and thus lead to an *increase* in the overall temperature of the planet. At present, the Earth's temperature is predicted to increase by between 1°C and 5°C in the next 100 years. This will affect weather, sea levels, vegetation, habitats and biodiversity. Plans for ambitious projects to *monitor* and control the energy balance of the Earth have been on the drawing board for several years (Brand, 2007).

What is your opinion on human activity and global warming? What is the evidence connecting human activity with global warming? What can be done to change human activity? *Explain* your opinions in 500 to 600 words.

5.2.1 Global warming

We hear or see the words "Global Warming" on every corner. But (**1**) do we really know what is meant by global warming? To begin by introducing the facts (**2**). Our climate is warming and this does have (**3**) mostly negative impacts (**4**). Some suspicious (**4**) minds could think what has often been said (**5**), i. e. (**6**) that the recent warming is a part of the natural increases and decreases (**4**) of (**7**) Earth's temperature that happen (**3**) since ages (**4**). But (**1**) if we look at these ups and downs in the past, we can clearly see that the present increase of temperature is far exceeding (**3**) all the highest temperatures of the past. What is causing this increase? We note that (**7**) begin (**4**) of industrialisation matches with (**7**) begin (**4**) of the temperature increase (**5**). We (**8**) must agree that greenhouse gases, produced by burning fossil fuels, are (**7**) only *plausible* explanation for the temperature increase.

The effects of (**7**) predicted temperature increase could be worse that (**9**) we can imagine. The (**7**) desertification, which already lead (**3**) to famine (**10**) a huge number of people, will probably gain (**4**) territory and bring even more people (**5**) to death, to poverty or to refugee. The same could happen for the population living on coasts (**4, 11**). As the water level is predicted to *increase*, whole (**4**) countries on (**4**) coasts, especially those with low altitudes such as Holland or Belgium, will be under water (**12**). We could be witnesses to a huge migration caused by climate refugees. *Moreover*, the (**7**) animals and plants will have a similar *fate*. A great number of species will have to migrate to the more northern regions, and one million species are expected to be totally (**5, 13**) extinct. The polar ice masses, the (**9**) represent a big (**4**) part of world's water reserves could melt and cause a high level climatic disorder (**4**) by eliminating the Gulf Stream.

We have all (**4**) possible reasons to be alarmed and to take action. Here are some things we can do in every-day life. First, we can use less heat by turning down the heating in winter and turning off the air conditioning in summer. *Furthermore*, we can travel less by car and plane and more by bicycle and train. If we do have to use the car, we can choose a model with less possible (**4**) consumption or at least regularly inflate the tyres. We can also recycle the packing of the products we buy and prefer local products that don't (**14, 15**) require so much (**4**) transport. We can stop our (**5**) energy waste. And (**1**) the list is long.

But (**1**) the most important is to educate not only the masses but, above all, the children and try to make these changes not remain private (**14**) but make them be (**4**) part of politician's (**16**) thoughts and concerns in order to implement the needed (**4**) measures at the political and laws (**4**) level (**17**). For those who might be (**5**) concerned with (**7**) economical consequences of these measures, they should rather look into the recent rapports (**4**) of certain English economists, which (**18**) calculated even bigger (**4**) economical losses in case of not undertaking something for saving our resources (**5**). To sum up, I can only *cite* a great Indian proverb: "When Man will have (**3**) cut the last tree, killed the last animal and polluted the last clean river, he or she will notice that money cannot be eaten".

1 Avoid starting sentences with "and", "but", "because" or "so".
2 This is not a complete sentence. What did your grammar checker say?
3 The tense is incorrect.
4 Find a better word or expression.
5 Omit needless words.
6 Do not use abbreviations as part of the sentence.
7 Look at the guidelines for the use of "a" and "the" in box 1.5.
8 Make a better link.
9 Did you read your work?
10 Some words are missing.
11 It sounds like desertification could happen to countries on the coast. Improve the sentence.
12 Split this complex sentence into two new ones.
13 It is not possible to be more than extinct.
14 Make the sentence positive.
15 Always write out these forms.
16 The apostrophe for possession of a plural noun is almost always after the "s".
17 This sentence is too complex. Use three shorter sentences instead.
18 Use "who" when you are referring to people.

5.2.2 Global warming

Abstract

The *phenomenon* of global warming, the constant increase of the Earth's temperature, *correlates* well with the start of industrialisation. We must act now to prevent ecological catastrophes such as desertification and rises in sea levels. Education, especially of children, on the effects of global warming is the only way to ensure that governments implement the correct measures.

We hear or see the words "Global Warming" on every corner. However, do we really know what is meant by global warming? I begin by introducing the facts. Our climate is warming and this has mostly negative *consequences*. Some sceptical minds could think that the recent warming is part of the natural fluctuations of the Earth's temperature that have been happening since the beginning of time. If we look at these ups and downs in the past, we can clearly see that the present *increase* of temperature far exceeds all the highest temperatures of the past. What is causing this increase? We note that the start of industrialisation correlates with the rise in temperature. Thus, we must agree that greenhouse gases, produced by burning fossil fuels, are the only plausible explanation for the temperature increase.

The effects of the predicted temperature increases could be worse than we can imagine. Desertification, which has already led to famines and the starvation of a huge number of people, will probably cover further territory, causing even more deaths, more poverty and more refugees. Disasters could also happen to populations living on coasts. The water *level* is predicted to increase through global warming. Therefore, entire countries with coasts, especially those with low altitudes such as Holland or Belgium, will be under water. We could be witnesses to a huge migration caused by climate refugees. Moreover, animals and plants will have a similar fate. A great number of species will have to migrate to the more northern regions, and one million species are expected to become extinct. The polar ice masses, which represent a major part of world's water reserves, could melt and cause a high level climatic disturbance by eliminating the Gulf Stream.

We have every possible reason to be alarmed and to take action. Here are some things we can do in every-day life. First, we can use less heat by turning down the heating in winter and turning off the air conditioning in summer. Furthermore, we can travel less by car and plane and more by bicycle and train. If we do have to use the car, we can choose a *model* with the least possible consumption or at least regularly inflate the tyres. We can also recycle the packing of the *products* we buy and prefer local products that *require* less transport. We can stop energy waste. The list is long.

However, it is most important to educate not only the masses but, above all, the children. In addition, one should try to make these *changes* public so that they become part of politicians' thoughts and concerns. This should ensure that the *required* measures are implemented at the political and legal *levels*. For those concerned with the economical *consequences* of these measures, they should rather look into the recent *reports* of certain English economists, who calculated even heftier economical losses in case nothing is done. To sum up, I can only cite a great Indian proverb: "When Man has cut the last tree, killed the last animal and polluted the last clean river, he or she will notice that money cannot be eaten".

Exercise 5.2 invited you to discuss the contribution of human activities to global warming. Ecologists predict that global warming will cause temperatures to rise and thus threaten biodiversity. Imagine that you have been offered a post as a research scientist in a rain forest. It is your task to *compare* biodiversity in the protected part of the rain forest with the biodiversity found in deforested areas. You could perhaps compare the abundance of certain species in the two areas. The rich *variety* of life found in rainforests gives you plenty of choice. You could look at liana vines, orchids, parrots, toucans, monkeys, ants, flies, bacteria, fungi or even viruses.

Write your ideas in the form of a scientific manuscript. Use both a table and a *graph* to present your *observations* from the different areas. If you find yourself fighting with your software for making the table and plotting the graph, then you can always just do it by hand. Gregor Mendel, the father of genetics, recorded the weather for years by hand at his monastery in Brno. An article in "Nature" (Kemp, 2002) shows a table of Mendel's handwritten monthly weather reports. The author also discusses why both Mendel and Darwin used so few pictures in their works. If you are not sure whether a figure in your manuscript is *necessary* or not, think back to the habits of these two giants of biology. Would they have included your figure?

Documenting and measuring biodiversity are topics which are being actively pursued by many groups across the world. Discover the present status of *research* in these fields in articles from "Nature" (Stork, 2007) and "Science" (Zimmer, 2007).

5.3.1   Biodiversity of bacteria in rainforests

Biodiversity means (**1**) the great variety of species that has developed through evolution. This (**2**) biodiversity is no stable state (**3**), but (**2**) it changes (**4**) every day. New species are created (**5**); some species become extinct (**6**). This is the result of *destroying* habitats and the establishment of new habitats with different *conditions* for living (**7**). Very often, it is nature itself which can be blamed for this destruction. Unfortunately, the human species sometimes fastens (**1**) this naturally slow process. Therefore, over a short (**8**) time several species loose (**9**) their habitat and die out. The de-forestation of the rainforests is a good example of a human intervention that diminishes biodiversity.

To investigate the effect of deforestation on biodiversity in rainforests, we compared species (**8**) in an *intact* area of rainforest and a deforested area. We examined the bacterial flora because it reacts very fast (**1**) to changing conditions. Therefore (**10**), our investigation period only lasted (**3**) one year. We *investigated* (**1**) the *increase* in the number of different species in the bacterial flora of the soil. The results are shown in table 1 and graph 1 (**1, 11**).

Table 1 shows the development of the numbers of bacterial species in 1 m^3 soil over the investigation period of one year (**2, 12, 13**).

	Number of different bacterial species in 1 m³ soil	
	Area 1: intact rainforest	Area 2: deforested rainforest
01.06.01	25396	25456
01.07.01	25896	6697
01.08.01	25674	6536
01.09.01	24758	7643
01.10.01	23998	7904
01.11.01	24598	8630
01.12.01	25314	9004
01.01.02	25017	9762
01.02.02	24312	10536
01.03.02	23623	11985
01.04.02	24846	13025
01.05.02	25996	14624

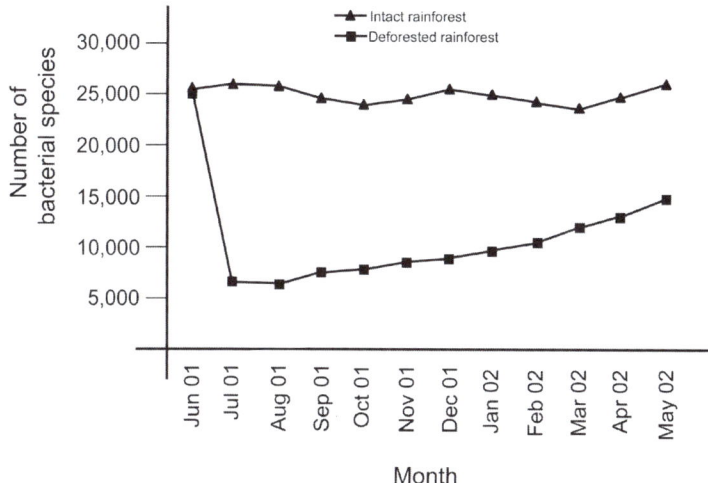

Month

Graph (**1**) 1 shows the strong *decrease* of bacterial species in 1 m³ soil after the deforestation of the rainforest in June 2001 (**12**).

In June 2001, the number of bacterial species was nearly equal in both areas. During June, the rainforest in area 2 was cut down. So, (**14**) the living conditions for bacteria changed rapidly: e.g. (**15**) more radiation of the sun (**1**) reached the ground and therefore, temperature increased (**16**). On the other hand, humidity decreased (**17**). This meant (**2, 18**) death (**1**) for the greatest part (**1**) of bacterial species in the soil. Graph (**1**) 1 shows this very clearly. In July 2001, we could (**2**) only identify 6700 different species of bacteria in 1 m³ soil. This means (**2, 18**) that nearly four fifths (**19**) of the population had died out.

Nevertheless, graph (**1**) 1 also shows that over the time situation recovered again. Until May 2002, biodiversity spread out again (**1**). The number of different species in the soil increased to nearly 15000 (**20**).

This examination (**1**) clearly shows (**1**) several points (**21**). Human behaviour can do (**2**) harm to (**2**) biodiversity and strongly diminish the variety of species in a habitat. It also shows (**22**) the facility (**23**) of nature to recover, as the increase in the number of species shows (**22**). Nevertheless, we must not ignore (**24**) that it takes (**4**) a long time until (**1**) the number of different species (**2**) will be as high as before the deforestation. *Consequently*, we should try to avoid any (**2**) harm to (**2**) nature and to protect biodiversity as far as possible (**2**).

1   Find a better word.

2   Omit needless words.

3   Improve this expression.

4   The tense is incorrect.

5   Avoid "created". It sounds like you believe in creationism.

6   This sentence needs improving.

7   This sentence needs improving and linking to the previous one.

8   Some words are missing.

9   This is a word that fools my spellchecker.

10 Find a better linking word.

11 This paragraph actually needs to be rewritten. I have provided an alternative in the corrected version.

12 Improve the titles of the table and the figure.

13 Table 1 contains much redundant information. How would you go about eliminating the redundancy?

14 Avoid starting sentences with "and", "but", "because" or "so".

15 Avoid using abbreviations as part of a sentence.

16 Split this sentence into two.

17 Put this information into the second sentence generated in (**16**).

18 Insert a linking word.

19 The use of fractions is correct. However, percentages are easier to understand and are therefore more common.

20 These three sentences do not fit together very well. Improve the situation.

21 If you say that there are several points, it is a good idea to list them.

22 The same word is found twice in one sentence.

23 This word is incorrect.

24 Positive sentences are easier to understand.

Abstract

We *compared* the number of bacterial species in intact and deforested areas of a rainforest. Deforestation led to the loss of 80 % of the species. One year after deforestation, the number of species had risen three-fold, indicating that the biodiversity could still be regained, albeit to a *limited* extent.

Biodiversity refers to the great variety of species that has developed through evolution. Biodiversity is not a stable state, it is changing every day. Some species are becoming extinct whilst new ones are arising. The extinction of species results from habitat destruction; the provision of new habitats with different living conditions permits new ones to arise. Very often, it is nature itself which can be blamed for this destruction. Unfortunately, the human species sometimes *accelerates* this naturally slow *process*. Therefore, over a short period of time, several species lose their habitat and die out. The deforestation of the rainforests is a good example of a human intervention that diminishes biodiversity.

To investigate the effect of deforestation on biodiversity in rainforests, we compared the number of species in an intact area of rainforest and a deforested area. We examined the bacterial flora because it reacts very rapidly to changing conditions. Consequently, our investigation was concluded within one year. We determined the increase in the number of different species in the bacterial flora of the soil. The results are shown in table 1 and figure 1.

Alternative to the above paragraph: To investigate the *effect* of deforestation on biodiversity in rainforests, we examined the *changes* in the bacterial flora of the soil. The rapid response of bacteria to environmental change allowed our investigation to be completed between June 2001 and May 2002. Table 1 and figure 1 *show* the number of bacterial species identified in two habitats during this *period*.

Table 1. Numbers of bacterial species in 1 m³ soil from June 2001 to May 2002.

| Sample date[1] | Number (in thousands) of different bacterial species in 1m³ soil | |
	Area 1: intact rainforest	Area 2: deforested rainforest
Jun	25.4	25.5
Jul	25.9	6.7
Aug	25.7	6.5
Sep	24.8	7.6
Oct	24.0	7.9
Nov	24.6	8.6
Dec	25.3	9.0
Jan	25.0	9.8
Feb	24.3	10.5
Mar	23.6	12.0
Apr	24.8	13.0
May	26.0	14.6

1   All measurements were made on the first day of each month.

Note on corrections made to Table 1: The first column was simplified by specifying the time *period* in the title and the time of measurement in the footnote. The second and third columns were simplified to three significant figures and by giving the numbers as thousands.

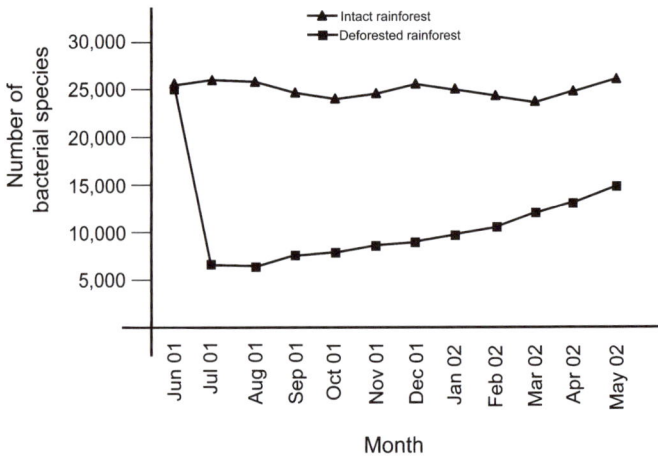

Figure 1. Number of bacterial species in 1 m³ soil of the rainforest between June 2001 and May 2002.

In June 2001, the number of bacterial species was nearly *equal* in both areas. During June, the rainforest in area 2 was cut down. *Thus*, the living *conditions* for bacteria changed rapidly. For instance, more solar radiation reached the ground, leading to an *increase* in soil temperature and a *concomitant decrease* in humidity. Consequently, the majority of the bacterial species in the soil perished. Figure 1 shows this very clearly. In July 2001, we identified only 6,700 different species of bacteria in 1 m³ soil. Thus, nearly 80% of the population had died out.

Figure 1 also shows that, in spite of the *extensive* loss of species, the number of species began to rise again and biodiversity began to return. At the start of May 2002, the number of different species in the soil had *increased* to nearly 15,000.

This investigation clearly *illustrates* several points. First, human behaviour can harm biodiversity and strongly *diminish* the *variety* of species in a habitat. Second, the increase in the number of species shows the ability of nature to *recover. Nevertheless*, we must realise that it will take a long time before the biodiversity will be as high as before the deforestation. Consequently, we should avoid harming nature and protect biodiversity.

5.4   Stereotypic Man

Women have been and still are underrepresented in science. Many programs have been initiated to correct this *imbalance*. In my course, with a majority of female students, discussions about the value of such programs as well as their *chances* of success or failure are usually lively. Here is the text (taken from "Goodbye Tarzan: Men After Feminism" by H. Franks) that I use to initiate discussions on the subject. Note the lack of formal English and the many words that are not found in scientific manuscripts.

Box 5.1   Stereotypic Man

While feminists have pointed out how trivialising and restricting stereotypic *images* are on the lives of women, it seems to have escaped most men's notice that they are trivialized and restricted too.

"Man and machine in perfect harmony", goes a car commercial on television, implying more than its originators realize. Do men really want to be as smooth-running and predictable as machines? Surely not in real life. But how do they resist when they are sold glamorous irresistible packages? The cool guy who never shows emotions but smokes a cigar instead …the superman, fast-living, risk-taking, getting admiring gasps from lesser mortals … the James Bond smoothie who's quick on the draw … the beer-swilling hero who knows how to live rough, no frills, no fuss. Heroes all, and all guaranteed to get the girl (even though in real life terms they display potentially reckless or violent behaviour, considerable repression and give every indication of becoming unrewarding lovers and companions).

And in contrast, there are the failure symbols, the warning signals to laugh at … the swot with glasses, the clumsy thickhead, the henpecked, the weedy, ineffective, accident-prone wimp. Some stereotypes can become manipulative tools: to get out of the housework, there's the lost little boy, can't do a thing for himself, but who is still so loveable and a wow with women. And another type is the "perfect husband", who gets on with being the breadwinner and taking the dog for a walk, neither sissy nor sexy, the sober, production-line man – using his perfection in lieu of passion and involvement.

These images *affect* men's behaviour and women's expectations. There is the father *image*, stern and uncommunicative or *sensitive* and uncommunicative, or violent and uncommunicative. And the divorced father, indifferent to his family, busy making it with younger women. There is the manager, ruthless whiz-kid, the irresistible "bastard". The good pal, beer-swilling, telling dirty jokes. And the doctor, remote and kindly – we're back to the uncommunicative man again.

These are not easy images to emulate and they have rather a bad effect, both on those who can actually live up to them, and those who can't.

Women as well as men have been brainwashed into accepting the standards created by these characters. Unfortunately, those traits billed as most desirable are the kind most women would be better off without – aloofness, tantalisingly hard to get, controlling, never admitting weaknesses. Versions of this sadistic figure turn up in movies, on television, in romantic fiction. What kind of promise do TV coppers or James Bond offer in the way of meaningful relationships? Yet they are the unsmiling, inhuman hero figures that men have been taught to emulate and women have been taught to regard as desirable. (Reprinted by permission of A. Franks)

I found this text in the workbook "In Advance" by R. Side. One of the questions posed by Mr. Side on the extract is whether its author is male or female (Question reprinted by permission of R. Side). The students in my course enjoy discussing this point. Generally, the female students think the text was written by a man whereas the male students think that the text was written by a woman. What is your opinion? State the reasons supporting your opinion in less than 300 words. In the previous edition, a former student recommended an on-line tool called "Gender Genie" to differentiate between texts written by males and females (based on work by Argamon et al., 2003). Unfortunately, this intriguing tool is no longer accessible. In this edition, the corresponding manuscript has been replaced by one that purports to look at "Stereotypic Man" from both a male and a female viewpoint. Read both viewpoints and decide whether these viewpoints themselves were written by a man or a woman.

5.4.1 Stereotypic Man: is the author of this article male or female?

In my opinion (1) the author of this article could be of either gender. I will first state arguments for a male (2), then for a female author (2) and (3) finally (1) I will explain my personal decision.

Arguments for a male author (I call him James):
James finds it unfair that there is made so much fuss (4) about the stereotypic images of women by feminists breathing revenge, (3) whereas (5) in his opinion (5) men are just as often victims of these trivialisations. He therefore (2) decides to write an article unrevealing (2) the pressure put on men from stereotypes present in out (6) everyday life. In this manner (1) he wants to show everyone that men are exploited in just the same way (7), in conclusion (2) that they experience an equal treatment.

Being a man himself, James can easily name many different characters (2) of male stereotypes and give many examples for them (7). He can feel (2) with other men who are forced into stereotypes as he has experienced this himself many times. He does not have to meditate long in order to name examples: (8) this can be (7) observed by the articles (6) fluent style.

James has also paid attention to other men's behaviour, and he (7) has observed that many of those men eagerly try to emulate a stereotype, very often not even consciously. He **(9)** also noticed that many women literally force men into these roles as stereotypic models, thus falsifying their **(10)** conception of men as well.

However, it is surprising is that James does not talk in particular about the effects these stereotypes have on men **(3)** whereas an article about women would certainly add a list with **(7)** topics such as depression, bulimia etc **(2)**.

Arguments for a female author (I call her Linda):

Linda wrote this article in order to correct an image many feminists have and **(2)** she thinks is false. She wants to show everyone **(7)** that men are just as often victims of stereotypy **(2)** as women are **(7, 11)**.

Unfortunately, she forgot to mention why this is so, **(3)** but it is a well-known fact **(7)** that women talk more frankly about weight problems and low self-esteem than men do **(3)**, this again for the same reason as treated **(7)** in the article, the stereotype of men is strong, untouchable and very well able to handle any kind of problems without help from the outside. Talking about the effect of stereotypes on men would reveal weakness where there is not supposed to be any **(7)**.

Linda has become neutralized to those stereotypic characters over the years **(3)**, she thinks that it is rather ridiculous that there are **(7)** women falling for them. She is capable of **(7)** very quickly uncovering **(2)** such behaviour **(2)** and orders **(2)** them **(10)** in a long list with many examples.

Another motivation to write this article for her was her **(7)** knowing many women who have suffered from men emulating stereotypes **(3)** and she **(10)** hopes to motivate these women to take **(12)** the men's pressure.

Linda is engaged in equalizing the rights of men and women. There has certainly been and there is still a lot of **(13)** work to do in **(2)** women's rights. However, discovering abuse of men should not be forgotten.

My personal decision

I think it is **(7)** a male author having written **(14)** the article because of the following sentence: "... it seems to have escaped most men's notice that they are trivialized and restricted too."

The author clearly addresses **(14)** men **(3)**, and it seems more obvious **(2)** to me that a men **(6)** is writing for other men than an women **(15)**. A woman would write for everyone, as the stereotypic man is as much a problem for men as for women.

1 Look at the use of commas, situation 3, in section 1.2.2.1.
2 A word is missing or the present one needs improving (e.g. big, do, make).
3 Sentence is too complex. Keep it simple; try just one idea per sentence.
4 The sentence structure is incorrect.
5 Look at the use of commas, situation 2, in section 1.2.2.1.
6 Be more careful in reading your work.
7 Omit needless words.
8 Do not use the colon like this.
9 The tense is inconsistent.
10 What does the pronoun (e.g. it, they, this, that, these) refer to?
11 Why is there a paragraph break here?
12 Is this what you mean?
13 Avoid "a lot", "lots", "a bit" and similar diffuse expressions.
14 The tense is incorrect.
15 This is unclear. Place the final expression earlier in the sentence.

5.4.2 Stereotypic Man: is the author of this article male or female?

In my opinion, the author of this article could be of either gender. I will first state arguments for a male author, then for a female one. Finally, I will explain my personal decision.

Arguments for a male author (I call him James):

James finds it unfair that so much fuss is made about the stereotypic images of women by feminists breathing revenge. However, in his opinion, men are just as often victims of these trivialisations. Consequently, he decides to write an article uncovering the pressure put on men from stereotypes present in our everyday lives. In this manner, he wants to show everyone that men are similarly exploited, that is that they experience an equal treatment.

Being a man himself, James can easily name many different forms of male stereotypes and give many examples. He can empathise with other men who are forced into stereotypes as he has experienced this himself many times. He does not have to meditate long in order to name examples as can be observed by the articles' fluent style.

James has also paid attention to other men's behaviour, and has observed that many of those men eagerly try to emulate a stereotype, very often not even consciously. He has also noticed that many women literally force men into these roles as stereotypic models, thus falsifying women's conception of men as well.

However, it is surprising is that James does not talk in particular about the effects these stereotypes have on men; in contrast, an article about women would certainly list topics such as depression and bulimia amongst others.

Arguments for a female author (I call her Linda):

Linda wrote this article in order to correct an image many feminists have that she thinks is false. She wants to show that men are just as often victims of stereotyping as women. Unfortunately, she forgot to mention why this is so. However, it is well-known that women talk more frankly about weight problems and low self-esteem than men do because, as in the article, the stereotype of men is strong, untouchable and very well able to handle any kind of problems without help from the outside. Talking about the effect of stereotypes on men would reveal weakness none should be.

Linda has become neutralized to those stereotypic characters over the years. Indeed, she thinks that it is rather ridiculous that some women fall for them. She can very quickly reveal such types of behaviour and arrange the types in a long list with many examples.

Another motivation to write this article for her was knowing many women who have suffered from men emulating stereotypes. Linda hopes to motivate these women to resist men's pressure.

Linda is engaged in equalizing the rights of men and women. There has certainly been and there is still much work to do for women's rights. However, discovering abuse of men should not be forgotten.

My personal decision

I think a male author wrote the article because of the following sentence: "... it seems to have escaped most men's notice that they are trivialized and restricted too."

The author is clearly addressing men. Hence, it seems more likely to me that a man rather than a woman is writing for other men. A woman would write for everyone, as the stereotypic man is as much a problem for men as for women.

Scientists have the reputation of being rational and analytic think-ers, permanently seeking after elusive truths. In reality, *of course*, they are people first and scientists afterwards. They can be as emotional as any non-scientist, ready to throw their toys out of their prams at the slightest irritation. One common emotion found amongst scientists is professional rivalry. Michael White has written a book putting forward the *hypothesis* that rivalry is the force that drives scientists to publish their results (White, 2001). Envy is another emotion frequently shown by scientists. The extent of professional envy was captured many years ago in a wonderful cartoon in the "New Yorker" magazine. Two cavemen watch a third caveman walk-ing towards them. The first caveman says, "Look, that's the man who discov-ered fire!" The second one replies, "True, but what has he done since then?"

This exercise *asks* you to imagine that you are the person who discovered fire. You have been criticised for starting global warming. Nevertheless, you wish to press ahead and optimise fire production to reduce wood con-sumption and lower carbon dioxide emissions. *To this end*, you have been *trying* to improve the quality of fires by testing different woods with *various* properties. Write a manuscript on your results to show the world that you continued to be scientifically *active* after your world-shattering *discovery*.

5.5.1   Finding the best firewood to make fire

Introduction

Fire is a tool which can provide good (**1**) service to humans. But (**2**) it also exposes us to danger. We might (**1**) be hurt or even killed by fire when it is not treated with the respect it deserves. Therefore, it is very important (**1**) for us to receive (**1**) as many (**3**) information about its properties as possible. Increasing our knowledge and understanding of the nature of fire will help us to live with it in a way full of comfort and pleasure (**4**). For example, we will be able to heat our caves and furthermore we will be able to (**4**) warm our food and roast our meat.

Here (**5**) we demonstrate that the quality of fire depends on the material used for burning (**4**). We *compare* the influence of different plants on (**6**) fire and prove (**7**) the importance of the state (**4**) of the conditions of the plants.

Materials and Methods

Standard procedures were used for collecting wood. Cutting of the wood (**4**) was done as described previously. A list of plants used in this study is given in Table 1.

Results

Different plants – different fire

For our experiments, we used the branches of four different plants, listed in (**4**) Table 1. These branches were cut to equal (**8**) pieces. This uniformity made sure (**4**) that the quality of fire depended on the kind of the plant and not on the size of it (**4**). As fireplace we chose a planar (**3**) area in a cave, to be sure that the wind conditions could not change during and between the experiments (**9**). The fireplace (**8**) was surrounded by stones. The fire was inflamed (**1**) according to the (**8**) protocol. After counting to hundred by our countperson ten pieces of the cut branches were thrown into the flames (**9**). We observed how much the fire swelled on (**4**) and *documented* how many counts it took till (**1**) the fire seemed to extinct (**3**). Before it went out (**1, 5**) we added again ten pieces of the same plant and *repeated* our observations (**10**). This procedure was done (**1**) five times, with all different (**4**) plants tested. As shown in Figure 1 (**4**) we could demonstrate for the first time, (**5**) that the branches of Biggy are the best firewood, *followed* by Sharpy and (**5**) to a lesser extent (**5**) by Whitey. Although the branches of Spikey *induced* the same reaction of the flames as Whitey did (**11**), this plant is not recommended to (**3**) use as firewood. Burning of Spikey results in a thick, black smoke, which causes shortness of breath and tears in the eyes.

Same plant, different conditions – different fire

In this *experiment*, we investigated the role of the *condition* of the firewood. The same plants as in the experiments desribed (**12**) previously were used. 20 branches were put (**1**) for ten days into water, 20 branches were put for the same period in the sun and 20 branches were stored in the cave (**4, 13**). For the experiment (**5**) the same conditions as in the upperwritten (**3**) one (**4**) were chosen. All 20 branches, either the wet or the dry one (**4**), were thrown into the fire and the reaction of the flames were observed. The results were very surprising. We could show that wet firewood is *detrimental* to fire. Using wet wood led to the death of the flames. (**13**) Using the firewood stored in the cave the results agreed with the results obtained previously. But (**2**) using the very dry firewood, which laid

(**3**, **14**) in the sun for ten days, its effect on fire was magnificent (**9**). The flames went straight to heaven for approximately 1 to 2m and the fire kept burning for twice the time it did when normal firewood was used (**4**).

Discussion

In this study, we reported (**14**) the importance of choosing the right (**1**) firewood for making fire. We showed (**14**) the advantage of using branches of Biggy and warned (**14**) of the danger using branches of Spikey. *Furthermore* (**5**) we could *shed light on* the different effects of the various conditions of firewood. We *postulate* that the best firewood is very dry firewood. Therefore (**5**) we recommend to collect (**3**) as much firewood as possible, lay (**1**) it into the sun for at least two weeks and store (**3**) it in a very dry cave protected by many thick (**8**) hides.

Table 1. Plants used in our experiments.

Common name	Description
Whitey	Tree, ~ 10m high, white bark, green small leaves
Sharpy	Tree, ~ 30m high, brown-black bark, green needles
Biggy	Tree, ~ 100m high, brown bark, big green leaves
Spikey	Shrub, ~ 2m high, many thorns

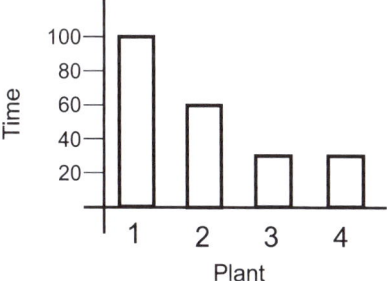

Figure 1. Measuring (**10**) of the time (by counting from 1 to 100) between throwing 10 pieces of the tested plant into (**15**) fire and the almost (**8**) disappearance of the last flame. (1) Biggy, (2) Sharpy, (3) Whitey, (4) Spikey.

1 Find a better word.
2 Avoid sentences starting with "and", "but", "because" or "so".
3 This word is incorrect.
4 Omit needless words.
5 Look at the use of commas in section 1.2.2.1.
6 Some words are missing.
7 Use "prove" only for theories and laws. See box 3.6.
8 A word is missing.
9 This sentence needs rewriting.
10 This expression can be improved.
11 Write this sentence more directly.
12 Use your spellchecker.
13 The order of the experiments performed should be the order in which you report the results. Report the results with the confirmatory ones first (i. e. from the cave). Continue with the ones showing new data.
14 The tense is incorrect.
15 "The" is needed. Without it, you appear to be writing about the universal "fire".

5.5.2 Finding the best firewood to make fire

Abstract

We recently reported on the great *discovery* of fire. We showed how to ignite a fire by rubbing a specially *prepared* branch with a sharp stone. Here, we have determined the type of branch that generates the best fire and how best to prepare branches for burning.

Introduction

Fire is a tool which can provide excellent service to humans. However, it also exposes us to danger. We can be hurt or even killed by fire when it is not *treated* with the respect it deserves. *Therefore*, it is vital for us to obtain as much information about its properties as possible. Increasing our knowledge and understanding of the nature of fire will help us to live with it comfortably and pleasurably. *For example*, we will be able to heat our caves, warm our food and roast our meat.

Here, we *demonstrate* that the quality of fire depends on the material used. We compare the *influence* of different plants on the generation of fire and demonstrate the importance of the conditions of the plants used.

Standard procedures were used for collecting wood. Wood cutting was done as described previously. A list of plants used in this study is given in Table 1.

Results

Different plants – different fire

For our experiments, we used the branches of four different plants (Table 1). These branches were cut to equally sized pieces. This uniformity ensured that the quality of fire depended on the kind of the plant and not on its size. To ensure that the wind conditions could not change during and between the experiments, we chose a level area in a cave for the fireplace. The fireplace itself was surrounded by stones. The fire was ignited according to the previous protocols. Our countperson counted to 100. Then, ten pieces of the cut branches were thrown into the flames. We observed how much the fire swelled and documented how many counts it took before the fire seemed extinguished. Before it died completely, we added again ten pieces of the same plant and observed the fire's behaviour. This procedure was repeated five times with each plant tested. We could demonstrate (Figure 1) for the first time that the branches of Biggy are the best firewood, followed by Sharpy and, to a lesser extent, by Whitey. The branches of Spikey induced the same reaction of the flames as Whitey did; nevertheless, this plant is not recommended for use as firewood. Burning of Spikey results in a thick, black smoke, which causes shortness of breath and tears in the eyes.

Same plant, different conditions – different fire

In this experiment, we investigated the *role* of the condition of the firewood. The same plants as in the experiments described previously were used. 20 branches were placed for ten days into the cave, 20 branches into water and 20 branches in the sun. For the experiment, the *conditions* described above were chosen. All 20 branches from each treatment were thrown into the fire and the reaction of the flames were observed. The results with the firewood stored in the cave agreed with those obtained previously. The results obtained with the wet wood, however, were very surprising. Wet wood *caused* the death of the flames and was thus detrimental to fire. In contrast, the very dry firewood, which had been placed in the sun for ten days, had a magnificent effect on the fire. The flames went straight to heaven for approximately 1 to 2 m and the fire burnt for twice as long as observed under standard conditions.

Discussion

In this study, we report the importance of choosing the suitable firewood for making fire. We show the advantage of using branches of Biggy and warn of the danger using branches of Spikey. Furthermore, we could shed light on the different effects of the various conditions of firewood. We postulate that the best firewood is very dry firewood. Therefore, we recommend collecting as much firewood as possible, placing it in the sun for at least two weeks and storing it in a very dry cave protected by many thick animal hides.

Table 1. Plants used in our experiments.

Common name	Description
Whitey	Tree, ~ 10m high, white bark, green small leaves
Sharpy	Tree, ~ 30m high, brown-black bark, green needles
Biggy	Tree, ~ 100m high, brown bark, big green leaves
Spikey	Shrub, ~ 2m high, many thorns

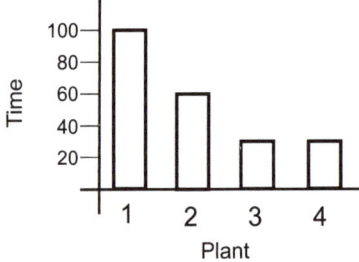

Figure 1. Measurement of the time (by counting from 1 to 100) between throwing 10 pieces of the tested plant into the fire and the almost complete disappearance of the flame. (1) Biggy, (2) Sharpy, (3) Whitey, (4) Spikey.

5.6 Is there a connection between eating organic food and cigarette smoking?

The *idea* for this exercise originated in Denmark. I noticed during my stay in the pretty town of Aarhus that organic foods were enjoying widespread popularity. The yoghurt and the jam served in my hotel at breakfast were all organic as was the beer and food at the nearby Café Mozart. Indeed, the organic foodstuffs and beer were important to the marketing strategy of the café. I was less clear on the Mozart connection as there were no pictures of him on the walls and the music was mostly from Cuba. I started to wonder whether Mozart might have been a pioneer of organic foods.

Throughout my stay, I was impressed by this devotion to healthy sources of food and drink. I was, however, singularly unimpressed by the air quality of the café which was thick with cigarette smoke. It seemed on some evenings that I was the only one not smoking. I wondered why people who were so conscious about their sources of food and alcohol would not think about stopping smoking. The *situation* was the same in the beautifully furnished breakfast room in my hotel. Everyone was keen on the organic breads and jams, but most guests decided to accompany their breakfast with a heart-starter (English for an early morning cigarette).

I think it is time for a *survey* to find out whether there is a positive correlation between eating organic food and smoking. Do the majority of people who eat organic food also smoke? Is it just those who drink organic beer who smoke? Was I just unlucky and the victim of a statistical anomaly? Do people eating organic food think that non-organic food really is more dangerous than smoking? Have all the restaurants which sold organic food but which did not allow smoking gone out of business? Is there a market for organic tobacco?

Your task is to select some of the above questions and imagine how people might reply. Describe the *analysis* of the replies in a scientific *report*.

5.6.1 Fogged Minds

Introduction

It is well established that smoking has *detrimental* effects on our health by causing *severe* diseases such as heart attacks or lung cancer. Consequently, it should (**1**) be assumed that sane people would stop smoking, but currently it seems as if the number of smokers is increasing (**2**).

However (**3**), beside (**3**) this soaring auto-aggressive behaviour (**4**) an interesting development concerning the demand for wholesome food has taken place in the last few years (**5**). Considering (**3**) the smoking behaviour of our society (**4**) this seems quite controversial, because on the one hand, people carry on (**1**) to commit suicide in instalments whereas on the other hand, they long for organic food to ameliorate their health and to prolongate (**6**) their lives (**7**). To elucidate (**1**) this paradox (**4**) we decided to survey smokers who attach importance to organic food about their motivation to smoke (**7**).

Methods

We created (**1**) a questionnaire which should shed light on the *partici-pants* (**8**) smoking and nutrition (**1**) behaviour as well as on their social status and leisure time activities. 250 persons at (**1**) the ages of 16 to 65 participated in this study. To evaluate the collected data (**4**) particular (**1**) statistical methods were applied.

Results

According to our data (**4**) 30 % of the respondents stated (**1**) to smoke more than 20 cigarettes a day. Only 15 % of the participants smoke less than 5 cigarettes a day. There is a strong correlation between the ages and the daily consumed cigarettes (**9**). On average (**4**) young people, especially adolescents, smoke more than older people (data not shown).

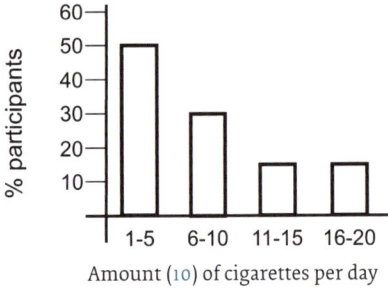

Figure 1: Amount (**10**) of cigarettes per day. Cigarette amount (**10**) is displayed on the x-axis. The y-axis denotes for the percentage of participants who smoke this particular amount (**10**).

The *reasons* for smoking are manifold and astonishing. More than one third of the interviewed smokers do (**11**) not even know why they are smoking (**11**). *Moreover*, 18 % of these persons do (**11**) not even like the taste of a cigarette. In general, the main reason for smoking was to dispose (**1**) of stress. Even 70 % of the participants aged 16 to 20 mentioned this point as cause for (**9**) smoking.

78 % of the interviewees are (**11**) aware of the negative effects smoking exhibits (**9**) on their health and had at least tried once to stop smoking.

Only 22%, mostly people who smoke less than 10 cigarettes a day, do (**11**) not believe that their smoking is more unhealthy than (**4**) for example (**4**) breathing the polluted air of big (**1**) cities. In particular, smoking seems not to be a question of the (**12**) social status as no correlation between the cigarette amount (**10**) smoked and the social circumstances could be determined.

Considering the nourishment, 75% of the persons *exclusively* live on organic food whereas the remaining 25% attach great importance to wholesome products (**7**). In addition, 64% of the *participants* regularly do sports. 62% of the respondents seriously believe that they can avoid the negative effects of smoking by consuming organic food. 38% agree that organic food is just a good excuse to stick to their smoking habits.

Discussion

In this survey (**4**) we tried to elucidate the controversial behaviour of smoking and simultaneous consume (**1**) of organic food. Our results again bring alarming evidence that smoking in fact (**1**) is a *severe* addiction as many people seriously tried (**11**) to stop smoking but did not succeed in (**5, 9, 13**).

The invention (**1**) of organic food even seems to aggravate this development (**1**), because many smokers seriously (**14**) believe that consumption of organic food can ameliorate (**1**) the negative effects of smoking. Paradoxically, it seems as if these (**15**) new awareness of wholesome nutrition *supports* smoking. Therefore, it would be necessary to intensify anti-smoking campaigns. Especially young people (**16**) should be informed about the severe effects smoking exhibits (**1**) on their health.

1 Find a better word.
2 Improve sentence construction and use a better linking word.
3 Find a better linking word.
4 Look at the use of commas in section 1.2.2.1.
5 Omit needless words.
6 Use your spellchecker.
7 This sentence is too complex. Split it into two new ones.
8 An apostrophe is missing.
9 Improve this expression.
10 Note the difference between "amount" and "number".
    See box 5.2 for some examples.

11 The tense is incorrect.

12 "Social status" covers this concept worldwide. "The" is therefore not required.

13 Make the sentence positive.

14 The word "seriously" appears in the previous sentence. Find an alternative for this sentence.

15 Did you read your work? Did you notice what your grammar checker said?

16 Avoid starting sentences with "especially".

Box 5.2 Number, amount, volume and concentration

I am surprised how often students use these words incorrectly. To clarify the meaning of these words, this box presents an imaginary set of questions from a mentor to a mentee.

Please tell me the number of times that you have repeated this experiment. Which amount in grams of sodium chloride did you weigh out? Which volume in litres of water did you add to the sodium chloride? What was the final concentration in grams per litre of the solution?

5.6.2 Fogged minds

Abstract

We have investigated the smoking behaviour of 250 people who regularly eat organic food. 85 % of the interviewed people smoked at least five cigarettes per day; 30 % of the interviewees smoked more that 20 cigarettes per day. 62 % believed that organic food would prevent the negative effects of smoking, *suggesting* an unexpected *reason* for eating organic food.

Introduction

It is well established that smoking has detrimental effects on our health by causing severe diseases such as heart attacks or lung cancer. Consequently, it might be assumed that sane people would stop smoking; however, it seems currently as if the number of smokers is increasing.

Nevertheless, in addition to this soaring auto-aggressive behaviour, an interesting development concerning the demand for wholesome food has recently taken place. Given the smoking behaviour of our society, this seems quite controversial. On the one hand, people continue to commit suicide in instalments whereas on the other hand, they long for organic food to *ame-*

liorate their health and to prolong their lives. To *investigate* this *paradox*, we decided to survey smokers who attach importance to organic food. Specifically, we wanted to learn about the factors motivating them to smoke.

Methods

We devised a questionnaire which should *shed light on* the participants' smoking and nutritional behaviour as well as on their social status and leisure time activities. 250 persons between the ages of 16 to 65 participated in this study. To *evaluate* the collected data, selected statistical methods were applied.

Results

According to our *data,* 30 % of the respondents admitted to smoking more than 20 cigarettes a day. Only 15 % of the participants smoke less than 5 cigarettes a day. There is a strong correlation between the age and the number of cigarettes consumed daily. On average, young people, especially adolescents, smoke more than older people (data not shown).

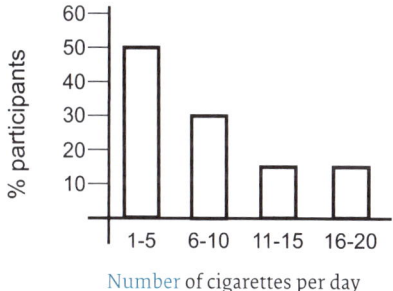

Figure 1: Number of cigarettes per day. Cigarette number is displayed on the x-axis. The y-axis denotes for the percentage of participants who smoke this particular number.

The reasons for smoking are manifold and astonishing. More than one third of the interviewed smokers did not even know why they smoke. Moreover, 18 % of these persons did not even like the taste of a cigarette. In general, the main reason for smoking was to reduce stress. Even 70 % of the participants aged 16 to 20 mentioned this point as a reason for smoking.

78 % of the interviewees were aware of the negative effects that smoking has on their health and had at least tried once to stop smoking. Only 22 %, mostly people who smoke less than 10 cigarettes a day, did not believe that their smoking is more unhealthy than, for example, breathing the polluted air of large cities. In particular, smoking seems not to be a *question* of social status as no correlation between the number of cigarettes smoked and the social circumstances could be determined.

How does the nutritional behaviour influence smoking? 75 % of the persons exclusively live on organic food, whereas the remaining 25 % attach great importance to wholesome *products*. In addition, 64 % of the participants regularly do sports. 62 % of the respondents seriously believe that they can avoid the negative effects of smoking by consuming organic food. 38 % agree that organic food is just a good excuse to stick to their smoking habits.

Discussion

In this survey, we tried to elucidate the *controversial* behaviour of smoking and *simultaneous* consumption of organic food. Our results again bring alarming *evidence* that smoking is indeed a severe addiction as many people have seriously tried to stop smoking but failed.

The development of organic food even seems to aggravate this problem, because many smokers earnestly believe that consumption of organic food can lessen the negative effects of smoking. Paradoxically, it seems as if this new awareness of wholesome nutrition supports smoking. Therefore, it would be necessary to intensify anti-smoking campaigns. Young people especially should be informed about the *severe* effects smoking has on their health.

Here are the six most frequent commands and comments I made to the students' texts in this chapter. As in chapter 3, I counted similar comments (e.g. "improve this word" and "improve this expression" as well as the comma comments for this chapter) as the same. Keep these six comments in mind when redacting your own work.

▮ A word or expression is missing or the present one needs improving.
▮ The sentence structure needs improving or the sentence is too complex.
▮ Look at the use of commas in section 1.2.2.1
▮ Omit needless words.
▮ A linking word is required.
▮ Use a spellchecker or check your spellchecker.

5.8 Take-home messages from Chapter 5

Ten essential editing commands
1. Read your work several times.
2. Verify the paragraph structure.
3. Ensure that all sentences relate to each other logically.
4. *Verify* that all sentences are complete.
5. Shorten and simplify sentences that are too long or too complex.
6. Carefully check the tenses.
7. Identify words or expressions that could be improved.
8. Examine carefully all linking words.
9. Verify the usage of words that you are employing for the first time.
10. Omit needless words.

Articles

Brand, S. (2007) Earth Monitoring: Whole Earth Comes into Focus. Nature **450**, 797.

Haag-Wackemagel, D. (1993) Street Pigeons in Basel. Nature **361**, 200.

Kemp, M. (2002) Peas without Pictures: Gregor Mendel and the Mathematical Birth of Modern Genetics. Nature **417**, 490.

Stork, N.E. (2007) Biodiversity: World of Insects. Nature **448**, 657.

Zimmer, C. (2007) Predicting Oblivion: Are Existing Models up to the Task? Science **317**, 892–893.

Books

Franks, H. (1984) Goodbye Tarzan: Men After Feminism.

Side, R. (1994) In Advance.

White, M. (2001) Rivals: Conflict as the Fuel of Science.

Websites

Argamon, S., Koppel, M., Fine, J. and Shimoni, A.R. (2003) Gender, Genre and Writing Style in Formal Written Texts.
www.cs.biu.ac.il/-koppel/papers/male-female-text-final.pdf

No-one collects data without stopping to think what it means.
P. B. MEDAWAR

I mentioned in chapter 4 (page 98) that the planning and construction of a manuscript really begins with the generation and analysis of the data itself. Would it therefore be feasible to commence writing a manuscript at the same time as an experiment is being performed? Let us investigate this notion, assuming that you are treading loosely the path known as "the scientific method". You have chosen the scientific problem that you wish to investigate and have done some background reading to help you formulate a hypothesis. The first experiments have been planned and are about to be executed. A manuscript seems far away, like a mirage on the horizon. Is it though? Is a manuscript perhaps nearer than you think?

I think it is, with the connection to the manuscript going through the records you keep in your notebook or your laboratory journal. Your supervisor will, I hope, have impressed upon you the importance of recording everything that you do and observe. The reasons given might include ensuring priority for a patent application or the fulfilment of the legal obligations of your institute. In addition, I also explain to my students that accurate record-keeping is essential to prepare a successful experiment for inclusion in a thesis or a manuscript. Conversely, in the case of failure, it can help to ascertain the reason(s) why something did not work as planned.

Regardless of success or failure, it will be necessary to clearly explain why you did an experiment, how you did it and why you set up the subsequent one. Such explanations are the quintessence of scientific communication. You need to be able to relate what you did first to yourself and then to other scientists. Above all, you need this skill when an experiment fails to go according to plan or gives an unexpected result. How can you expect your supervisor or colleague(s) to counsel you if you cannot explain in a series of straightforward and logical terms what you actually did?

It is here that the connection between doing research and writing becomes most tangible. Explaining the preparation, execution and analysis of an experiment is like writing a manuscript. The background needed to understand why you did something is the introduction, the execution is the methods and the analysis forms the results and discussion. Box 6.1 illustrates this idea by detailing how I might have explained to a colleague a problem that I was having in setting up the system to measure influenza virus in the model manuscript in chapter 4. Decide for yourself whether you think that this is a short manuscript or not.

Box 6.1 Explaining an experimental problem to a colleague

I am trying to set up a system using canine kidney cells to measure influenza virus particles. I want to see whether any of my plant extracts contain substances that inhibit influenza virus reproduction. I have been growing the cells in culture dishes of 1 cm diameter at 37°C in a commercial medium, adding the virus and looking for surviving cells after 2 to 3 days. I see evidence of viral reproduction because the cells die in the presence but not in the absence of virus. However, the problem comes when I try to quantify the extent of reproduction. I either see that all the cells in a dish are destroyed or that all of them survive. There is nothing in between so that I cannot detect subtle reductions in the number of virus particles. Is it possible that I need more cells in the dish for the amount of virus being added? Could it be that I should use culture dishes of 2 cm diameter so that I obtain more cells?

In my view, explaining to yourself or your colleagues why you did something or why you selected one particular experimental approach over several others is not only a vital step in communication but also perhaps the most crucial skill required for mastery of the scientific method. It is the first step in the analysis and interpretation of the outcome of an experiment or a series of experiments. Over the years, I have concluded that young scientists, independent of origin and field of study, find this part of the scientific method very taxing.

Here are two pieces of evidence to support this view. The first was collected during the supervision of one of my first Master's students in Vienna. The student would greet me in the morning with the dispiriting comment, "Es ist nicht gegangen" ("It did not work"). It was relatively easy to make him wait with his daily pronouncement until I had drunk my first coffee of the day; however, I had much more trouble teaching him that the expression "It did not work" is negative and meaningless because it is absolutely no use in finding out what the problem was and thus pointing a way to a solution. I tried to support him by always posing the same questions (Was there no signal? Was the signal too small, too large or different from what he usually obtained? Had he changed anything from the previous experiments?), but he remained steadfast in repeating "It did not work". The absence of any constructive analysis demonstrated that the scientific method had escaped him.

The second example has its origins in a frustrating encounter a colleague of mine had with one of her graduate students. The experiments they had planned had not worked out as expected. Together, supervisor and student had tried to find out the reasons but were unable to pin them down. What lay behind this inability? In the view of the supervisor, the student lacked the capacity to analyse and interpret the data scientifically. In the student's opinion, it was the supervisor's responsibility to introduce the student to an understanding and application of the scientific method. Conflicts like these between graduate students and supervisors occur with a depressing regularity. The resulting discontent on both sides, coupled with slow or no progress, frequently leads to taut relationships.

Writing up experiments as you go and learning how to explain the execution of an experiment will save time during the post-mortem of a failed experiment and shorten the time needed for successful troubleshooting. Discussing this process in more detail is not really within the scope of this book, but I would like to mention two points for you to consider. Experience has shown that they help to troubleshoot more rapidly and thus accelerate your project and/or provide you with more time for writing.

First, remember that the explanations for many failures are simple ones deriving from human nature. There are innumerable stories about institutes calling in the repairman to fix a machine that had simply not been switched on or about an apparent breakdown of a computer network resulting from a window cleaner's ladder that had inadvertently disconnected a cable. Eliminate such trivialities as rapidly as possible.

Second, it is important to avoid assumptions as to where to look for the source or sources of the problem. This is idea is exemplified by the anecdote of a man who lives on the 33rd floor of a block of flats. When he travels up to his flat with the lift, he takes the lift to the 30th floor and then climbs the stairs to the 33rd floor. On the way down, he always takes the lift from the 33rd to the ground floor. What is the reason for this peculiar behaviour? Is it connected with what happens when the man takes the lift on the way up or is it due to what happens on the 30th or 33rd floors? People who find the solution immediately do so by imagining what happens when someone calls a lift. Those who take longer concentrate on all sorts of situations that might arise at the 30th floor. These colleagues then receive the hint that the man travels directly to the 33rd floor when he travels with another person. This is a clear indication that that the problem concerns the man and his interaction with the lift. Certain people still continue to ignore the initial part of the experiment. To me, this has to be considered poor scientific analysis. (By the way, in case you are still wondering about the solution, the man is too small to reach the button for the 33rd floor, but he can manage to press the button for the 30th floor. If the man travels with someone else, he or she will press for the button for the 33rd floor for him. On the way down, the man can reach the button for the ground floor without any difficulty.)

In summary, the main thrust of this brief chapter is that the execution, description and communication of experiments are closely intertwined. Keeping this in mind will improve both your scientific communication and your abilities as an experimental scientist.

Take no notice of what your elders tell you.
MAX F. PERUTZ

This book is about learning and applying the conventions used in scientific writing. They became established many years ago and have changed little over time. The advice in this book is designed to help you adhere to these conventions, thus preventing *conflicts* with the scientific community and saving you time and energy in writing manuscripts. This final piece of advice *suggests* ways to extend the basics that were presented in the previous chapters. Here are some approaches to identifying new directions for structuring sentences, expressing thoughts and encountering new words.

One key approach is to briefly *analyse* scientific papers that you read. Make a note of sentence constructions or words that are new to you and store them as *possibilities* for the future. *Ask* yourself the following questions. How clear were the main conclusions? Was a particular section difficult to understand? If so, what were the *reasons*? Would you have written the sentences in the same way as in the paper? Remember that a text can always be written in a different way.

In section 4.3.3 on p107, I suggested that, when preparing the references, you should not stop the flow of writing to look for a particular reference. This strategy of not stopping can also be applied to writing the text itself. In other words, just keep writing without stopping to check for the spelling of a word or for a synonym. Forget about the fine sentence structure and the most optimal linking word, just aim for the completion of a section or a chapter of your text. Research has shown that this strategy is preferred by many non-native speakers when they write a text in English.

Once you have a first draft, you can start to improve it using the resources such as a dictionary or a thesaurus listed in section 7.1. The other resources may also be able to supply you with ideas on how to make your text more mature by shortening it or be introducing more appropriate words. Whichever you choose, this active process of challenging your writing will certainly have a positive outcome on the quality of your text.

Another idea for refining writing technique is to read scientific articles and books that are not directly related to one's *research*. The science journals "Science" or "Nature" are a good place to start. Each week, these journals have articles of general interest that take about 15 minutes to read. Eight examples of such articles that I use in my course, each coupled with a task for you, are mentioned in chapter 8.4. Some of these general interest articles are available on-line without charge. If not, there should be access to these journals via the computers in your university computer room, department or library.

If you have more time for reading, have a look at the list of 78 books in section 7.3. Many of the books concern the lives of scientists or discuss a scientific theme. Some touch on major themes of today such as evolution, the environment and the origins of emerging viruses. Certain books were deliberately chosen because they create or fuel controversy.

An excellent example of scientific controversy was the acrimonious debate on the nature of evolution between Stephen Jay Gould and Richard Dawkins. Kim Sterelny (Dawkins vs Gould: Survival of the Fittest, book 53 in the list) explains the scientific *background* to the controversy and *compares* the theories and opinions that led to their disagreements. The controversy, despite the ferocity, was *nevertheless* a discussion based on *interpretation* of evidence obtained through scientific processes. Many other controversies are, however, not based on scientific *evidence*. It is important to read about such discussions and learn to *refute* arguments that lack a scientific *basis. To this end*, the book list contains two books to support you in this task. Both examine current problems facing our world, one from a non-scientific and one from a scientific, fact-based viewpoint.

Not all the books in section 7.2 have an explicit relationship to science. Indeed, the choice of some of the books as sources of words to extend your scientific writing or vocabulary may surprise you. Experience shows, though, that new words for your scientific vocabulary can be found in any text, provided that you are looking out for them. As an *illustration*, read the five lines on the nature of love from Shakespeare's Romeo and Juliet in box 7.1. The nine words highlighted in blue will *strengthen* the vocabulary of any young scientist.

It does not, therefore, matter what you read to improve your writing. The important thing is that you encounter, store and actively use new words. In addition, you should, at least some of the time, analyse the way in which a text is written. Here is a final set of questions to *consider* whilst reading. Which type of sentence does a writer use? How does a writer link his or her sentences together? Could you write in the same style as your favourite writer? Do you think the writer was thinking about how a text

would appear to the reader? This is the most important question of all.
Successful writing is best achieved when the writer tries to put him- or
herself into the position of the reader.

Finally, section 7.4 links to four videos to support you in your oral presentations

Box 7.1 Words from Shakespeare for use in scientific writing

Here is a delightful text from Shakespeare's Romeo and Juliet.
"Love is a smoke raised with the fume of sighs;
Being purged, a fire sparkling in lovers' eyes;
Being vex'd, a sea nourish'd with lovers' tears;
What is it else? A madness most discreet;
A choking gall and a preserving sweet."

Romeo and Juliet (I, i) (http://shakespeare.mit.edu/romeo _juliet/index.html)

The words in blue are useful for scientific writing. Here are some
sentences that *illustrate* their use.

▌ Cigarette smoke contains hundreds of different chemicals.
▌ Volatile solvents are stored in a fume cupboard.
▌ Traffic fumes are a major source of air pollution.

What is the difference between smoke and fumes?

▌ Many medicines are available to purge the intestines.
▌ Purge the incubator after use to remove any traces of oxygen.
▌ Why do diamonds sparkle?
▌ *Poorly* nourished children will fail to grow.
▌ Companies try to be discreet about their projects to prevent competi-
tors from gaining an advantage.

Note the word "discrete" which looks similar but has a quite different
meaning.
▌ Atoms are made up of discrete particles.
▌ Pumps in nuclear reactors often have a choke to regulate the water supply.

▌ Gall is a body fluid which is required to digest fat in the human intestine.

▌ Very low temperatures preserved the body of the Tyrolean ice-man.

7.1 Resources

Dictionaries

1. Advanced Learner's Dictionary (Oxford).
2. Collins English Dictionary (Collins).
3. Shorter Oxford English Dictionary (Oxford).
4. http://dictionary.com
5. Yahoo widget dictionary

Thesauri

6. Oxford Dictionary and Thesaurus (Oxford). This combination of dictionary and thesaurus manages both tasks well.
7. Cassell's Thesaurus (Cassells).
8. Roget's Thesaurus (Tophi).
9. http://thesaurus.com
10. www.wordwebonline.com

Resources for writing

11. **The Elements of Style** by William Strunk, Jr. and Elwyn B. White (Macmillan). This book is an absolute classic. It is the guiding light for my writing.

12. **The Complete Stylist and Handbook** by Sheridan Baker (Crowell). If you want more detail than in Strunk and White, then this is the book for you.

13. **The Elements of Editing: A Modern Guide for Editors and Journalists** by Arthur Plotnik (Macmillan). Here are plenty of useful tips on how to write accurately.

14. **The Penguin Guide to Punctuation** by R. Larry Trask (Penguin). This short book presents punctuation in an extremely clear way. If you hate commas, semi-colons and their friends, this book may change your mind.

15. **Modern English Usage** by Henry W. Fowler (Wordsworth Editions). Here is another author dedicated to *concise* and accurate writing. Many writers call this book their Bible for writing as it provides answers to almost all questions about written English.

16. **Errors in English (and Ways to Correct Them)** by Harry Shaw
(Barnes and Noble). Mr. Shaw shows how to correct errors in grammar, punctuation and spelling. I find the guide to correct sentence structure extremely useful.

17. **Usage and Abusage: A Guide to good English (Abusus Non Tollit Usum)** by Eric Partridge (Penguin). Are you *confused* by the *difference* between "assume" and "presume" or by "affect" and "effect"? This book will aid you in sorting out your difficulties. Have a look at the section entitled "brevity". It will provide you with another approach to omitting needless words.

18. **In Advance** by Richard Side (Nelson). This is the book in which I found the text "Stereotypic Man" (section 5.4). It is full of similarly stimulating exercises to make you think how to plan and create clear and concise texts.

Resources for writing and speaking scientific English

19. **Communicating in Science: Writing a Scientific Paper and Speaking at Scientific Meetings** by Vernon Booth (Cambridge). This little book, not quite so old as "The Elements of Style", is also a classic. The content is presented concisely and remains topical. The section recommending the use of overhead transparencies is perhaps the only part that seems out-of-date.

20. **How to write and publish a scientific paper** by Robert A. Day and Barbara Gastel (Oryx). Robert Day was an editor of the Journal of Bacteriology who was unhappy with the standard of the manuscripts that were submitted for publication. His *solution* was to write this book, aimed at both novices and experienced scientists.

21. **An Outline of Scientific Writing: For Researchers with English As a Foreign Language** by Jen T. Yang and Janet N. Yang (World Scientific). In contrast to the previous book, this one is designed for those who have not grown up speaking English.

22. **Writing Technical Reports** by Bruce M. Cooper (Penguin). Why do we immediately think a technical *report* will be boring to read? Mr. Cooper's approach shows that this need not be the case.

23. **Dazzle 'em with style: The Art of Oral Scientific Presentation** by Robert R. H. Anholt (Elsevier). Are you looking for support in preparing your next scientific seminar? Do you want to find out how to transform the figures from your manuscript into legible slides? Here are plenty of examples to point you in the right direction.

Resources for finding and handling references

24. **Pubmed**, www.pubmed.gov

25. **ISI Web**, http://isiwebofknowledge.com

26. **Google scholar**, http://scholar.google.com

27. **Scopus**, https://www.scopus.com

28. **A database of all databases in medicine and related sciences**, www.meddb.info

29. **Endnote**, www.endnote.com

30. **BibTex**, www.bibtex.org

31. **Medlars**, www.nlm.nih.gov/bsd/mmshome.html

Background to the English Language

34. **The Professor and the Madman: a tale of Murder, Insanity and the Making of the Oxford English Dictionary** by Simon Winchester (Penguin). If you think dictionaries are boring, then read this book. You will never look at a dictionary the same way again.

35. **Mother Tongue: The English Language** by Bill Bryson (Penguin). Are you *interested* in learning more about the language you are using? This is then the book for you. I found the chapter on how English is used in non-English speaking countries most amusing. I wonder constantly at the new combinations of English words that Austrians generate.

36. **Frantic Semantics: Snapshots of our Changing Language** by John Morrish (Pan). Mr. Morrish selects 150 commonly used words and examines how their meanings have changed over the years. *Follow* the evolution of a language as it happens.

37. **www.krysstal.com/borrow.html** Enjoy this never-ending collection of words that English has borrowed from other languages.

38. **www.etymonline.com** If you want to rapidly find the origin of a word that you have just discovered, this is a good place to start.

Over the years, I began to make a list of the most common comments that I make when correct students' writing in my courses. Eventually, I found I had one page with 33 numbered comments that I could give to the students as a handout at the beginning of term. When correcting their texts, I just needed to write down the number of the comment. This was clearer for the student and saved me time in marking. To further help the students, I also added the page number of this book on which they could find out the background to the comment. Any further comments needed for a particular text could be added by hand. The texts in section 5.1.1 and 5.4.1 were corrected using these collated commands, just numbered according to appearance to suit the format of the chapter.

I have included my latest version of this list in Box 7.2 to support you in editing your work. The page numbers refer to this third edition of the book.

Box 7.2   My current thirty-three comments for correcting texts

1   Use a spellchecker or check your spellchecker. (p17)
2   Not a complete sentence. Always write complete sentences
    with correct punctuation. (p21)
3   Comma guideline 1. (p22)
4   Comma guideline 2. (p22)
5   Comma guideline 3. (p22)
6   Comma guideline 4. (p23)
7   Why did you set commas here? (p22)
8   Do not use the colon like this. (p23)
9   Avoid the dash, use commas or brackets instead. (p25)
10 Avoid using abbreviations as part of the sentence. (p25)
11 Always write these forms out. (p25)
12 Do not start sentences with "and", "but, "because" and "so".
    Use better joining words. (p25–26)
13 Do not end sentences with "too", "also", "though", "yet or similar linking
    words. (p26)
14 A linking word is needed. (p26)
15 Avoid "get". (p27)
16 Avoid "a lot", "lots", "a bit" and similar diffuse expressions. (p27)

17 This is not a word in the English language (p17). What did your spellchecker say?

18 A word is missing or the present one needs improving (e.g. big, do, make). (p32)

19 Avoid this word. (p32)

20 Indent your paragraphs. (p39)

21 There are problems with the paragraph structure. (p39)

22 Why is there a paragraph break here? (p39)

23 Sentence is too complex. Keep it simple; try just one idea per sentence. (p39)

24 Make sentence more direct; see how much more powerful it is (p40).

25 Omit needless words. (p43)

26 Be more careful in reading your work. (p45)

27 What do you mean? (p45)

28 Improve your text with suggestions and questions in Box 3.2. (p55)

29 Place adverb close to the verb. (p55)

30 What does the pronoun (e.g. it, they, this, that, these) refer to? (p55)

31 Proband is not used in this way in English. (p73)

32 Nothing can be proven experimentally. (p78)

33 No capitals for chemicals (p67)

7.3 A reading list to improve your vocabulary and your scientific writing

How wonderful to be able to read the thoughts of others.
MICHAEL C. SUMMERS

Here is a list of 78 books, divided into groups. I chose the entries on the list primarily because I thought they might *interest* young scientists wishing to improve their vocabulary and their written English. I also selected them to *promote* discussion, debate and argument. Some of the books are controversial and should give you practice in debunking pseudoscience and refuting irrational arguments.

I recommend that you try at least one of the first three on the list. Ernst Mayr's book is one of the most clearly written books on evolution that I have read. The other two are excellent for honing your debating skills on controversial subjects.

1. **One Long Argument: Charles Darwin and the Genesis of Modern Evolutionary Thought** by Ernst Mayr (Penguin). In 164 pages, Ernst Mayr expertly summarises 150 years of debate, presents Darwin's five theories and discusses why these theories have encountered so much opposition. This book explains the fundamentals of Darwinism clearly and succinctly.

2. **All the Trouble in the World: The Lighter Side of Famine, Pestilence, Destruction and Death** by P. J. O'Rourke (Picador). Mr O'Rourke attacks almost every position of the so-called "enlightened" world, including scientific ones such as global warming and biotechnology. If you do not agree with his propositions and contentions, how would you set about persuading him otherwise?

3. **Factfulness: Ten Reasons We're Wrong About The World - And Why Things Are Better Than You Think** by Hans Rosling, Ola Rosling and Anna Rosling Rönnlund. With this book, you can challenge your beliefs, your assumptions and your interpretation of everyday statistics about the world. Perhaps we can be optimistic about the future if we are prepared to give up our prejudices.

On scientists

4. **On Giant's Shoulders: Great Scientists and Their Discoveries from Archimedes to DNA** by Melvyn Bragg (Sceptre). Melvyn interviews the famous about the thoughts and insights of great scientists. Read the comments of Dawkins, Gould and Maynard-Smith on Darwin's life and writings, ponder on reasons why the Greeks chose to do science and learn how Poincaré *demonstrated* that chaos could arise from apparently rigid laws.

5. **The Double Helix: A Personal Account of the Discovery of the Structure of DNA** by James D. Watson (Longman). Love them or hate them, Watson and Crick's proposal of a structure for DNA changed the world.

6. **What Mad Pursuit** by Francis Crick (Basic). Francis Crick did not just *propose* a *structure* for DNA. He also predicted the existence of mRNA, tRNA and coiled-coil protein structures. What did the symmetry of the crystals of DNA tell Crick about DNA structure?

7. **Rosalind Franklin: The Dark Lady of DNA** by Brenda Maddox (Harper Collins). Rosalind Franklin did not just produce beautiful diffraction patterns of DNA. She also carried out outstanding work on the properties of coal and investigated the molecular *structures* of tobacco mosaic virus and poliovirus.

8.   **Memoirs of a Thinking Radish: An Autobiography** by Peter B. Medawar (Oxford). Will I ever achieve his style? How can I learn to use words as he did?

9.   **Surely, You're Joking, Mr Feynman!: Adventures of a Curious Character** by Richard P. Feynman and Ralph Leighton (Vintage). I mentioned in section 5.5 that scientists are people first and scientists second. Feynman is a perfect example. Wonder at the personality of a true genius. By the way, are you worried about giving your first scientific talk? Then wonder at the scientists who attended Feynman's first talk and realise that your audience cannot be as daunting.

10.   **Einstein in Berlin** by Thomas Levenson (Bantam). Why did Einstein become and *remain* a superstar? Be prepared for a surprise when you learn who chose Einstein's second wife for him.

11.   **The Life of Isaac Newton** by Richard Westfall (Canto). Find out about Newton's dispute with Leibniz and the reason for Newton's knighthood.

12.   **Pasteur and Modern Science** by Rene Dubois (American Society for Microbiology). Watch Pasteur proceed from optically *active* crystals found in wine to a germ *theory* of disease.

13.   **The Statue Within: An Autobiography** by Francois Jacob and Franklin Philip (Cold Spring Harbor Laboratory). This book contains a thrilling description of the pleasure of discovering something new as well as many philosophical insights into science. Francois Jacob's first talk was memorable for the educational trick played by a colleague. Find the trick and imagine how you would have reacted.

14.   **Marie Curie: A Life** by Susan Quinn (Da Capo). This book has been praised as the definitive biography of this *remarkable* scientist. What sparked off the campaign to prevent the award of her second Nobel prize?

15.   **A Feeling for the Organism: The Life and Work of Barbara McClintock** by Evelyn Fox Keller (Freeman). Mendel worked on peas, McClintock worked on maize. Both were 30 to 40 years ahead of their time. Mendel was simply ignored. McClintock was treated as an outcast and openly insulted by her fellow scientists in a 20th century equivalent of a witch-hunt.

16.   **Leonardo: The First Scientist** by Michael White (Abacus). Michael White puts forward the interesting hypothesis that Leonardo da Vinci was the first experimental scientist. What do you think of the evidence he provides in support?

17. **England's Leonardo: Robert Hooke and the Seventeenth-Century Scientific Revolution** by Allan Chapman (Institute of Physics). How could one man do so many experiments in so many fields? This book is on the top of my pile of books to read!

On becoming a scientist

18. **I Wish I'd Made You Angry Earlier: Essays on Science, Scientists and Humanity** by Max F. Perutz (Cold Spring Harbor Press).In the last couple of decades, the reputation of science has become tarnished. Perutz argues for the importance of science in today's society and against those who try to denigrate it.

19. **Advice to a Young Scientist** by Peter B. Medawar (Basic). In his wonderful writing style, Medawar sets out to help young scientists set off on the right track. His short chapter on "What is Science" is one of the clearest I have read.

20. **Loose Ends** by Sydney Brenner (Current Biology). One of the few books I have ever bought twice. One of my esteemed colleagues ran off with my first copy. Uncle Syd gives his advice to young and old and compares the advice of Peter Medawar and Jim Watson.

21. **A PhD Is Not Enough: A Guide to Survival In Science** by Peter J. Feibelman (Perseus). Mr. Feibelman stimulates young scientists to think carefully on their future careers and urges reflection on the most effective approaches to achieve scientific goals.

22. **The Ascent of Man** by Jacob Bronowski (BBC). A personal favourite that helped me to decide to study a scientific subject. I still remember Bronowski's insights into the minds of Mendel and Pythagoras. His warm humanity remains an inspiration.

23. **Rivals: Conflict as the Fuel of Science** by Michael White (Secker and Warburg). This is the book mentioned in the exercise on fire in section 5.5 when I state that scientists are people first and rational thinkers second. After reading this book, I had the feeling that many of the greatest scientists never left their kindergartens.

192 On exploring worlds

24. **The Map That Changed the World: A Tale of Rocks, Ruin and Redemption** by Simon Winchester (Penguin). Simon walks the length and breadth of Great Britain to *test* a hypothesis on the origins of rocks that led to the beginnings of geology.

25. **Longitude: The True Story of a Lone Genius who Solved the Greatest Scientific Problem of his Time** by Dava Sobel (Harper Perennial). Discover how jealousy and ignorance *affected* the development and introduction of the 18th century equivalent of GPS.

26. **Into the Blue: Boldly Going Where Captain Cook Has Gone Before** by Tony Horwitz (Bloomsbury). Horwitz is exhausted by a week's sailing on a replica of Captain Cook's ship. Even with the 18th century equivalent of GPS, Horwitz is astonished that Captain Cook and his crew managed to find their way across the globe.

27. **The Discovery of Slowness** by Sten Nadolny (Gazelle Drake). Sten Nadolny looks at the lesser known English explorer John Franklin to derive guidelines for living in what we call modern times. Nadolny's basic tenet is to slow down and find the source of a problem before setting out to *solve* it.

28. **Zen and the Art of Motorcycle Maintenance** by Robert M. Pirsig (Vintage). In this cult book from the 70's, Pirsig crosses the USA on a motorcycle and, like Nadolny, derives guidelines for living in our society. Pirsig's central theme is to achieve excellence (as described by the Greek word "arete") by stepping back and *considering* problems as an entirety. Both Pirsig's and Nadolny's ideas can be used effectively in scientific writing.

29. **Nathaniel's Nutmeg** by Giles Milton (Sceptre). How did 17th century trade wars for spices lead to the renaming of one of the world's greatest cities?

30. **The Songlines** by Bruce Chatwin (Picador). Bruce Chatwin was one of the most charismatic travel writers in the second half of the last century. This book on the aboriginal culture in Australia is full of ideas on evolution, linguistics and anthropology and contains an interview with Konrad Lorenz. But how much does this book tell us about Chatwin himself?

31. **Into Africa: The Epic Adventures of Stanley and Livingston** by Martin Dugard (Bantam Press). Find out how an American journalist fought floods, infectious diseases and mutinies to find a Scottish needle in an African haystack.

32. **Dark Star Safari** by Paul Theroux (Penguin). Are you interested in
Africa? This is an excellent introduction to the continent, but decide for
yourself on the sources of the problems and possible *solutions*.

33. **What is Life?** by Erwin Schrödinger (Cambridge). A quantum physicist
explores the fundamentals of biology. Can we think of a gene as a quantum particle? Read Schrödinger's reasoning behind his idea.

34. **Cancer and Society** by John Cairns (Freeman). Published almost
30 years ago, this introduction to the nature of the terrible disease we call
cancer and its implications for society *remains* as topical and as accurate
as ever. This book should be required reading for every health minister in
the developed world.

On observing worlds

35. **The Affair** by C.P. Snow (House of Stratus). The story of an investigation into possible scientific fraud in a Cambridge college.

36. **The Cunning Man** by Robertson Davies (Penguin). An unusual doctor
and two curious Englishwomen provide a spritely introduction to medical English.

37. **The Silver Castle** by Clive James (Picador). A street boy from Bombay
philosophises on the differences between the English spoken by Japanese,
Germans, Americans and English. Clive James uses the novel to present
his witty observations on the present state of the English language.

38. **The Number One Ladies' Detective Agency** by Alexander McCall-Smith
(Polygon). This detective story with a difference is packed with useful scientific words and phrases.

39. **Cantor's Dilemma** by Carl Djerassi (Penguin). The father of the contra-
ceptive pill pokes fun at vain university scientists from across the globe.

40. **Code to Zero** by Ken Follett (Pan). This novel, based on the space race
and the cold war, will greatly enrich your scientific vocabulary.

41. **The Road to Wellville** by T. Coraghessan Boyle (Viking). This book,
recommended to me by one of my students, takes an ironic look at the
health and wellness industry around 1900. Little has changed in the last
hundred years.

42. **Youth** by John M. Coetzee (Vintage). If your project for your Ph.D. is
not going well, you may sympathise with the main character in this auto-
biographical story.

43. **A Very Decided Preference** by Jean Medawar (Oxford). Jean observes Peter's world and provides many wonderful insights.

44. **A Scientific Romance** by Ronald Wright (Anchor). What would you take with you on a trip 500 years into the future?

45. **The Longman Literary Companion to Science** edited by Walter Gratzer (Longman). Are you not impressed by any of my suggestions? Then browse through this fascinating anthology of scientific writing and see whether you can find something which appeals to you. Gratzer also reviews books for "Nature"; his reviews are themselves little gems of scientific writing.

On mathematics

46. **Alan Turing: The *Enigma*** by Andrew Hodges (Random House). Andrew Hodges portrays Alan Turing as the node connecting Gödel, Einstein, Feynman, Schrödinger in his "What is Life" phase and the origins of modern neurology. In my opinion, Turing's paper "On Computable Numbers" was a defining moment in 20th Century science.

47. **A Mathematician's Apology** by G. H. Hardy (Canto). The Canto version has a foreword by C. P. Snow with profound insights into the mind of one of the 20th century's most able mathematicians.

48. **Fermat's Last Theorem** by Simon Singh (Fourth Estate). Why did Fermat's last theorem take 350 years to *prove*? Will we ever know whether Fermat himself had a proof?

49. **The Man Who Loved Only Numbers: The Story of Paul Erdös and the Search for Mathematical Truth** by Paul Hoffman (Fourth Estate). An itinerant mathematician in an amphetamine rush travels the world solving mathematical problems and creating havoc in his friends' lives. Read how he consoled them by giving them an Erdös number.

50. **Evolutionary Dynamics: Exploring the Equations of Life** by Martin A. Nowak (Belknap). "The book of nature is written in the language of mathematics", Galileo observed. Nowak investigates equations describing viral dynamics, cancer and the development of linguistics. He has even looked at equations describing the evolution of English irregular verbs (Lieberman *et al.* (2007) Nature **449**, 713–716).

51. **Mendel (Past Masters)** by Vitezslav Orel (Oxford). I pass Mendel's former flat at Landstraßer Hauptstraße 30 on my way to work. There is no plaque. The ground floor is now a lingerie shop which I suppose has a remote connection to human heredity. This book, part of a fine series, provides the intellectual background and scientific atmosphere to Mendel's momentous work.

52. **The Tree of Life: Charles Darwin** by Peter Sis (Walker). Darwin's life and theories are explained in a series of beautifully drawn *illustrations*. Everyone starting a course on biology should read this book.

53. **Dawkins vs Gould: Survival of the Fittest** by Kim Sterelny (Icon). These two supporters of Darwinism were involved for 25 years in a raging controversy over the *mechanisms* of evolution and the importance of selection. Kim Sterelny *explains* why.

54. **Wonderful Life: The Burgess Shale and the Nature of History** by Stephen Jay Gould (W. W. Norton). Gould wonders at the organisms preserved in the Burgess Schale, an area in Western Canada, and interprets the meaning of the different fossils. Reading his views on evolution, it is extremely difficult to imagine why he argued so fiercely with Dawkins.

55. **On Growth and Form** by D'Arcy Thompson (Canto). Are there reasons why certain flowers have a *particular* shape? Do biological structures follow engineering principles developed by humans? The polymath D'Arcy Thompson offers answers to these and many others in this wide-ranging book.

56. **Acquiring Genomes: A Theory of the Origin of Species** by Lynn Margulies and Dorion Sagan (Basic). Both Lynn Margolies and Ernst Mayr *find* Darwin *vague* and confused on the definition of species and their origin. Lynn Margulies sets out her highly controversial ideas on how new species arise. What do you think?

57. **The Blind Watchmaker** by Richard Dawkins (Oxford). This book is less well known than "The Selfish Gene", but it is essential to understand the flawed logic found in the following book.

58. **The Edge of Evolution: The Search for the Limits of Darwinism** by Michael Behe (Free Press). A committed supporter of intelligent design puts forward flawed logic and ignores unpleasant evidence. Use your own thoughts as well as those outlined in "The Blind Watchmaker" by Richard Dawkins to refute the ideas in this book.

59. **Silent Spring** by Rachel Carson (Penguin). This book alerted a whole generation to the problems of insecticides and pesticides. Sadly though, even after 40 years, DDT remains our best weapon against the mosquitoes transmitting the agents that cause chikungunya, dengue fever and malaria.

60. **Naturalist** by Edward O. Wilson (Island). An autobiography of a Harvard biologist, museum curator and winner of two Pulitzer prizes, one for a book on ants. I kid you not. He describes one of the most important experiments ever performed whose outcome gives us hope that the human abuse of nature such as that described by Carl Hiaasen will be eventually reversible.

61. **Stormy Weather** by Carl Hiaasen (Pan). A comical crime story provides a platform for a vitriolic attack on those responsible for the destruction of Florida's environment.

62. **The Skeptical Environmentalist** by Bjørn Lomborg (Cambridge). Here is a voice against the Zeitgeist. Is global warming worth all the hot air it is generating?

On virology

63. **Viruses, Plagues and History** by Michael B. A. Oldstone (Oxford). Oldstone gives the background to the origin of the most important viral diseases and the methods available to fight them.

64. **Plagues and Peoples** by William H. McNeill (Anchor). A scholarly treatise on how humans offer pathogens opportunities and how pathogens dramatically *affect* human societies. I wonder how human genetics and human society in Africa are being shaped by the AIDS epidemic.

65. **Guns, Germs and Steel** by Jared M. Diamond (Vintage). Why did infectious diseases of humans originate mostly in Asia and Europe? Why are agriculture and infectious diseases connected? Why didn't the Incas conquer Europe? Diamond, though, has been accused of over-simplification by his fellow anthropologists. There is more on the debate at the "New York Times" at http://tinyurl.com/5vem3p.

66. **Catching Cold: 1918's Forgotten Tragedy and the Scientific Hunt for the Virus That Caused It** by Pete Davies (Penguin). How can we investigate an extinct virus? Can we *elucidate* what was special about the 1918/19 influenza virus? Could there be a repeat of this terrible pandemic?

67.   **Witness to AIDS** by Edwin Cameron (Tauris). A person taking triple therapy to combat AIDS movingly describes the background to the epidemic in South Africa.

68.   **And the Band Played on: Politics, People and the AIDS Epidemic** by Randy Shilts (Saint Martin's). Why did it take so long to recognise how the agent causing AIDS was transmitted? Learn about the complex mix of personalities and political views that delayed implementation of public health measures to stop this novel emerging virus.

69.   **The AIDS Pandemic: The Collision of Epidemiology with Political Correctness** by James Chin (Radcliffe). The author has an interesting story, but spoils it for me with incomplete sentences, needless words, and *incorrect* punctuation. I hope his epidemiology is more accurate. Always remember that errors in your manuscripts reflect on how you do your *research*.

70.   **28 Stories of AIDS in Africa** by Stephanie Nolen (Portobello). The perfect antidote to the denial, inaccuracies and attacks on rational scientific thought. Shouldn't we show the same courage in fighting unfounded thoughts as HIV-infected people do when fighting for their lives?

On the philosophy of science

71.   **Theory and Reality: An Introduction to the Philosophy of Science (Science & Its Conceptual Foundations)** Peter Godfrey-Smith (Chicago). Richard Feynman said that the philosophy of science is about as much use to science as ornithology is to birds. I disagree and offer this book as an excellent piece of evidence. How can we do science if we do not understand the processes behind it?

72.   **Logicomix: An Epic Search for Truth** by Apostolos Doxiadis and Christos H. Papadimitriou (Bloomsbury Publishing). An unusual presentation of the life and work of the great British philosopher Bertrand Russell.

Books on my desk

Since the second edition of this book was published, books on widely different subjects have piled up on my desk and in my bookshelves. I keep those that I really look forward to reading on my desk for inspiration. Here are six that are currently in front of me.

73. **The Origins of Knowledge and Imagination** by Jacob Bronowski. Based on a series of lectures in 1967 at Yale University, Bronowski brings together, in this surprisingly small book, science, language, the mind, knowledge, biology, physics, astronomy and mathematics to explain how intertwined our thoughts are about these subjects. It is another masterpiece to stand alongside his "Ascent of Man" (see book 22).

74. **The Invention of Nature: Alexander von Humboldt's New World** by Andrea Wulf. The Humboldt brothers Alexander and Wilhelm were two power-houses of German intellectual thought in the first part of the 19th century. Alexander von Humboldt explored South and Central America, mapping the New World, meeting a host of intriguing characters and setting up our modern vision of Nature.

75. **X, Y & Z: The Real Story of How Enigma Was Broken** by Dermot Turing. Alan Turing (see book 46) is generally regarded as the hero who cracked the Enigma code in the second world war. Written by Turing's nephew, this book looks at the Polish, French and German heroes who managed to obtain the code and operating instructions for the enigma machine and pass them on to the British.

76. **Vaccines: Are they Worth a Shot?** by Andrea Grignolio. The first two editions of "Writing Scientific English", referred to a book written by an AIDS denialist to stimulate arguments againt pseudoscience. In recent years, this debate has subsided to be replaced with one on the merits of vaccination, especially against measles virus. This book is a scholarly treatise on why so many people are against vaccination of (their) children against infectious diseases and how society can achieve higher rates of vaccination.

77. **The Age of Wonder: How the Romantic Generation Discovered the Beauty and Terror of Science** by Richard Holmes. Amongst this set of stories of the "second scientific revolution", there is a chapter that concisely describes the development of our modern scientific method and how writings about this method were to profoundly inspire the young Charles Darwin.

78. **The Tyranny of Metrics** by Jerry Z. Muller. Fed up with trying meet impossible milestones? Does every human activity have to be measured and quantified? If you answer yes to the first and no to the second question, this book is for you. Dare you pass it on to your university bigwigs?

As mentioned in section 3.4, presentations are also an integral part of my courses. To give you a flavour of these presentations, four previous participants agreed to be filmed giving three minute talks. You can connect to videos through the QR code below. Video 1 introduces the four speakers and their subjects (videos 2–5). In video 6, one of the speakers interviews me on how to successfully find a place in a research laboratory for an Erasmus stay abroad.

7.5   References

Books

Perutz, M.F. (1998) I Wish I'd Made You Angry Earlier: Essays on Science, Scientists and Humanity.
Shakespeare, W. (1595) Romeo and Juliet
   http://shakespeare.mit.edu/romeo__juliet/index.html

Variety is the very spice of life,
that gives it all its flavours.
WILLIAM COWPER

This chapter lists the words in this book that are printed in italics and the pages on which you can find them. Words from boxes 1.4 (linking words) and 1.7 (the basic scientific lexicon) appear in italics up to five times (section 8.1 and 8.2). Other useful words for scientific writing that are not contained in these boxes are printed once in italics (section 8.3). The lists, although extensive, cannot cover every word necessary for scientific writing. Expand the lists by carrying out the exercises from my course in section 8.4 and by adding words that you find useful when reading. Space is provided in section 8.5. When writing, try to use as many of the words from chapter 8 as you can. The more you *vary* your words, the livelier and more vivid your writing will be.

The QR code below takes you to two files on which you can hear the words of this chapter pronounced in British and American English.

8.1   Linking words

accordingly 94, 100, 107, 112	indeed 37, 61, 67, 104, 112
additionally 60, 91	instead 20, 26, 97
consequently 38, 55, 79, 123, 153	moreover 148, 170
for example 27, 40, 78, 116, 166	nevertheless 16, 55, 64, 157, 182
for instance 37, 40, 45, 92, 101	occasionally 30, 82, 95, 101
furthermore 55, 95, 121, 148, 165	of course 40, 52, 78, 105, 163
however 22, 39, 54, 59, 68	otherwise 39, 100
in addition 27, 28, 45, 96, 123	subsequently 118
in contrast 38, 55, 107, 116	therefore 57, 63, 108, 166
in short 46	thus 63, 80, 108, 113, 157
in summary 20, 108	to this end 112, 163, 182

Verbs

affect   59, 147, 158, 192
ask   109, 163, 181
attempt   89, 110, 137
cause   53, 127, 147, 167
cite   95, 119, 120, 148
compare   129, 151, 155, 163, 182
conclude   67, 108, 155
confirm   51
confuse   100, 185
consider   40, 64, 171, 182, 192
correlate   50, 61, 149
decrease   53, 68, 69
demonstrate   50, 74, 126, 166, 189
describe   24, 73, 138
destroy   147, 151
detect   17, 45, 52, 118
disprove   78
document   151, 164
explain   77, 83, 147, 195
find   45, 80, 122, 130, 195
follow   51, 117, 131, 164, 186
illustrate   54, 78, 115, 157, 183
increase   79, 90, 114, 148, 157
indicate   20, 105, 110, 131
induce   164
interest   114, 115, 186, 188
invent   72, 76
investigate   107, 133, 152, 173
judge   43, 92, 111, 129
observe   35, 111, 126, 132, 167
propose   109, 111, 189
prove   78, 116, 194
quantify   95
quote   119
remain   49, 53, 123, 190, 193
repeat   117, 123, 164
require   78, 117, 121, 150

search   65, 137
shed light on   165, 173
show   112, 127, 155
solve   75, 82
strengthen   55, 106, 182
suggest   105, 172, 181
support   90, 102, 119, 171
survive   129
test   78, 105, 107, 192
treat   119, 130, 166
try   62, 82, 90, 163
vary   66, 201
verify   117, 175
work   80, 90, 96, 101, 129

Nouns

absence   20, 30
analysis   62, 69, 98, 169
answer   97, 102, 123
appearance   28
application   25, 92, 122, 123
attempt   55, 115, 117
background   73, 78, 111, 119, 182
cause   57, 130
chance   77, 89, 93, 122, 157
change   122, 150, 155
citation   119
condition   118, 151, 157, 164, 167
conflict   181
consequence   77, 111, 149, 150
control   98, 131
data   63, 92, 98, 173
decrease   67, 153, 157
difference   66, 84, 134, 185
discovery   77, 82, 84, 163, 164
discrepancy   50
effect   49, 69, 123, 155
enigma   194

resistant   114
robust   133
severe   52, 169, 171, 174
significant   39, 44, 45, 54

similarly   21, 27, 50, 108
simultaneous   174
unable   39, 57

8.3   Words that extend the basic scientific lexicon

absolute   80
accelerate   155
accessible   107
achievement   122
adjust   125
ameliorate   172
amount   67
analyse   181
anticipate   106
approach   123
assess   133
assimilate   16
assumption   81
augment   30
basis   182
clarify   89
comprehensible   134
concise   184
concomitant   157
controversial   174
convey   48
delve   119
develop   129
deviation   104
devise   95
diminish   157
effectively   106
eliminate   74
elucidate   196
endeavour   76
envisage   129
equal   145
estimate   30

evaluate   173
extensive   157
fate   148
findings   117
gain   83
genuine   109
gradually   59
growth   76
identical   52
imagination   74
imbalance   157
impact   23
inaccurate   92
incidence   61
inconsistency   45
inevitably   76
influence   166
initiative   46
insight   81
insufficient   102
intact   152
interpretation   182
lessen   174
modify   106
monitor   147
novel   127
omission   101
perspective   79
phenomenon   149
postulate   165
potential   133
precise   113
predict   80

preliminary   127
prepare   166
primarily   93
probability   66
promote   188
property   112
protocol   167
rate   65
recover   157
redundancy   122
refute   182
reliability   100
remarkable   190
resolve   113
responsible   114
salient   51

sensitive   158
source   52
speculate   83
stipulate   121
succinct   115
superfluous   44
survey   169
system   100
technique   43
underestimate   61
vague   195
value   134
various   163
vital   115
worsen   62

8.4   Exercises using texts from Nature and Science

Here are eight texts that I use in my course. I chose them for this edition because they widen the students' vocabulary (a selection of important words from each are listed) and shed light on how science was or is done. There are also exercises associated with the texts to sharpen your talents of analysis and summary.

1. Cocaine and Freud (Rousseau, 2011)

Did you know that Freud's first publication was a monograph on the medical properties of cocaine? The monograph was based on his own experiences that led ultimately to his addiction to the drug. The book review "Giants on Coke" reviews a book on Freud's life with cocaine and compares Freud's attitude to his addiction to that of William Halstead, a surgeon from the USA who championed aseptic techniques.

Read the text and find the sentence containing the most thought-provoking question!

Useful words: niche, pillar, suppress, thrive, botch

2. Detonator of the population explosion (Smil, 1999)

Several exercises in this book concern global warming and energy supplies. Did you know that the Haber-Bosch process for the fixation of atmospheric nitrogen uses 1–2 % of the world's daily energy supply? The above Millenium Essay by Vaclav Smil describes the background to the invention of this process; abstract 8 in section 3.4.8 was a summary of the article. How would you summarise this article in less than 200 of your own words using different sentence structures? Yes, I know it is difficult but the exercise will help you learn how to summarise the background of your field for an introduction to a mansucript. The suggestions for avoiding plagiarism in chapter 3.2 should support you in this endeavour.

Useful words: ingenuity, pinpoint, momentous, unprecedented, assiduous

By the way, Vaclav Smil has some very interesting and occasionally idiosyncratic views on the energy supplies of the future and climate change. An interview in Science illuminates his ideas and describes the themes of his many books (Voosen, 2018).

3. Redacting with Mr. Darwin (Nickalls, 2009)

In this book, I have been at pains to encourage you to read and revise your written work. This piece examines the evolution of a text from Darwin over a period of twenty years. Eventually, the text was included in the "The Origin of the Species" and became a famous one that is often quoted. Examine the differences between the first text in 1837 and the final one in 1859. Which text do you think is most powerful? How many words from the first version are found in the final version? Which belief is found in the first text but is missing from the other three? Why was the elimination of this belief so important for Darwin's ideas?

Useful words: foreordered, inevitable, grandeur, infinitesimal, sublime

I am always amazed that Darwin could write the "Origin of the Species" without any knowledge of how traits are inherited. Indeed, Mendel's ground-breaking observation on inheritance in peas was not published until a few years after Darwin's most famous book. Jacob Bronowski's discussion of Mendel in his book "The Ascent of Man" (book 22 in the list in section 8.2) led me to think about the fundamental **differences** in the observations made by these two scientists. Can you summarise these differences in less than 50 words? Omitting as many needless words as possible, it is feasible to illustrate the differences in 10 words.

4. Teatime for Science (Finn, 2001)

A scientist from the USA reflects on a research stay at in a British laboratory and considers why the United Kingdom has such a high number of Nobel Prize winners. His conclusion: Teatime! Examine the author's arguments to see how strong his case is. Do you think you could introduce a general afternoon tea break in your institution? Can you identify any characteristics common to scientists in your country?

Useful words: ostensibly, jest, misguided, exhortation, contagious

5. Physics takes the biscuit (Fischer, 1999)

How would you introduce an equation from physics to the general public? Read how the science populariser Len Fischer successfully managed this task using the physics of biscuit dunking. Can you explain your current scientific project to general public in just five paragraphs?

Useful words: dunking, pastry, porous, shallow, counterintuitive

6. Red wine procyanidins and vascular health (Corder et al., 2006)

This article was referred to in section 4.3.1 as it has an example of an unconventional graph. A further question I ask my students about this text is whether the results shown support the authors' conclusions. What do you think? Here are some questions that you might like to answer to help you make a judgement on the manuscript. Why does the graph in Fig. 1d have a logarithmic scale? What information is available on the diet of the men who live longer? What is written about wine production in other areas of France with high levels of male longevity? What is the concentration of alcohol in wine compared to that of the polyphenols? As a reviewer, would you have recommended acceptance of this manuscript for publication? One of the videos in section 7.4 features a discussion by a former student on this paper. Do you agree with his point of view?

Useful words: longevity, potent, constituent, vasoconstriction, coronary

7. Mr. Bayes goes to Washington (Wang and Campbell, 2013)

If you build 249 houses in the same way and all of them stay up, you would say that the probability of the 250th house built in the same way staying up was rather high. If you visit a website every day, your browser will most probably prompt for this site when you type in a couple of letters of the URL. Such predictions were given a scientific basis by the Reverend Thomas Bayes in the 18th century. This book review describes the background to Reverend Bayes' ideas and the current use of his ideas in statistics and reasoning. Information used to make predictions with Bayesian statistics is known as a prior. The author of the book under review explains how priors were employed to accurately forecast the result of a U.S.A. presidential election. Use the internet to find other uses for Bayesian statistics and summarise them in less than 150 words. You will have to be concise!

Useful words: landslide, hardnosed, meandering, inference, priors

Here is an additional exercise for those of you familiar with the philosophy of Sir Karl Popper. How do you think Sir Karl would assess the probability of the 250th house staying up? Your answer should comprise at most two sentences!

8. Smooth Operator (Anon, 2105)

This short, whimsical Nature editorial on George Boole complements the above article on Thomas Bayes. Without Boolean algebra, searching databases such as PubMed would be much more complicated. Amazingly, Boole was without any formal education but was able to teach himself calculus and became a university mathematics professor. See if this text can help you understand the Boolean operators. Given that Tim Berners-Lee, the inventor of the html language, also has a surname beginning with the letter B, we should perhaps change our URLs from www to bbb to show our recognition of the contributions of Bayes, Boole and Berners-Lee to the development of the internet.

Useful words: prominent, shiver

Articles

Anon (2015) Smooth Operator. Nature, **527**, 8.

Corder, R., Mullen, W., Khan, N. Q., Marks, S. C., Wood, E. G., Carrier, M. J. and Crozier A. (2006) Red wine procyanidins and vascular health. Nature **444**, 566.

Finn, J. T. (2001) British Science: A Toast to Teatime. Science 293, 1589.

Fischer, L. (1999) Physics takes the Biscuit. Nature **397**, 469.

Nickals, R. W. D (2009) Evolution of the End of Origin. Science **326**, 801.

Rousseau, G. (2011) Giants on Coke. Nature **476**, 397.

Smil, V. (1999) Detonator of the Population Explosion. Nature **400**, 415.

Wang, S. and Campbell, B. C. (2013) Mr. Bayes goes to Washington. Science **339**, 758.

Voosen, P. (2018) The Realist. Science **359**, 1320–1324.

8.6   Words that you wish to add

Use the space on the subsequent pages to collect further useful words and phrases.

… an attempt to support students in their understanding of virology

Tim Skern
Coffee House Notes on Virology
2nd edition
facultas.wuv 2009, 198 pages
EUR 19,40 (D) / EUR 19,90 (A) / sFr 35,–
ISBN 978-3-7089-0532-7

Our knowledge of viruses and their relevance to disease is enormous. The diversity of viruses is fascinating, yet at the same time overwhelming. How can undergraduates of science and medicine begin to come to terms with scientific knowledge and viral diversity? "Coffee House Notes On Virology" is an attempt to support such students in their understanding of virology. The book contains the answers to 75 exam questions; written in a straightforward style. Each question was revised by students to ensure clarity and plain English. The book aims to stimulate interest in virology and encourage new students to go deeper into the subject.